To Bill Golden (1911-1959)
Herb Lubalin (1918-1981)
Paul Rand (1914-1996)
Reba Sochis (1911-1998)
Bob Gage (1921-2000)
Lou Dorfsman (1918-2008)
Steve Frankfurt (1931-2012)
Tony Palladino (1930-2014)
and Massimo Vignelli (1931-2014)

If you do it right,
it, *and you*,
will live forever

© Text and personal archives: 2015, George Lois.
© 2015 BIS Publishing
BIS Publishers
Het Sieraad
Postjesweg 1
1057 DT Amsterdam
T +31 (0)20 515 0230
F +31 (0)20 515 0239
www.bispublishers.nl
ISBN: 978 90 6369 399 2
Writer and Designer: George Lois
Digital Design and Composition: Luke Lois, Good Karma Creative

My name is George Lois. My father's father, and his
father's father and all those before them, are traced back to 265 BC
in ancient Greece when my name was originally
"Logos." In ancient Greek, "Logos" meant "word, reason, speech –
an actively expressed creative thought."
In the 6th century BC, the discovery of *Logos*, the act of speaking
by which the individual asserted his liberty, was the
seed of the birth of Democracy. Obviously, my earliest Greek ancestor
was a philosopher or orator – a wordmeister
with a gift for gab. As a graphic thinker, I claim my love for language
as a birthright; as an ad man and logotype designer,
my genes have helped make me the most word-driven art director
of our media age.

memorable brand name interacting
with a strong visual symbol to communicate a humanistic idea
is the ultimate art form in popular graphic communication. A Big Idea logo
that drives Big idea advertising, triggers visual recognition that
immediately sears a product's virtues into a viewers brain.

Nowhere in the oeuvre of the world of graphic design,
is everything I understand about the creative process more challenging
than in the creation of a brand name in the form of a logo.

The birth of a great logotype developed with a built-in, conceptual,
"catchy" brand name can visually impart information in
a nanosecond, delivering a specific ethos with a penetrating promise
of the power of the product – and has the potential of bringing
instantaneous success. (There are dozens of abstract, obtuse brand names,
visually presented with a meaningless geometric design, that
have been successful in world marketing, but only after many years of
advertising and promotion to communicate who and what they are.)

My goal is to create "humanistic" symbols, driven by a pregnant idea,
visualizing some recognizable aspect of the human experience and magically
relating it to a unique selling proposition...as well as the multitude of
possibilities of branding a Big Idea with an image...when you are denied the
opportunity to redesign a weak, uncommunicative logotype.

Most logos that have been designed in the world, are mindless.
Ultimately, the job of all advertising...is to brand,
and a Big Idea logo is the heart and soul of great marketing.

2015

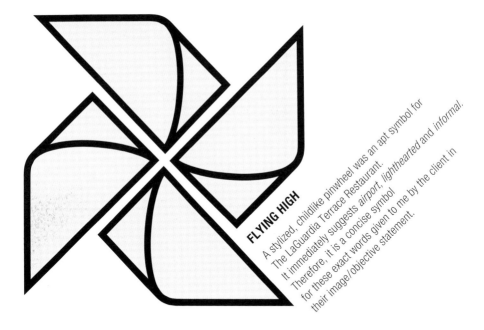

FLYING HIGH

A stylized, childlike pinwheel was an apt symbol for The LaGuardia Terrace Restaurant. It immediately suggests *airport*, *lighthearted* and *informal*. Therefore, it is a concise symbol for these exact words given to me by the client in their image/objective statement.

TO UPDATE LESTOIL,

I called it Tomorrow's Lestoil, and created an ad campaign starring a housewife in the 22nd century.

MY BABY BOOMER LOGO

AmericanLife TV programs to the Woodstock Generation who changed the world when they marched for racial equality, women's rights, and against the Vietnam War (usually wearing daisies to symbolize their peaceful Baby Boomer philosophy of Flower Power).

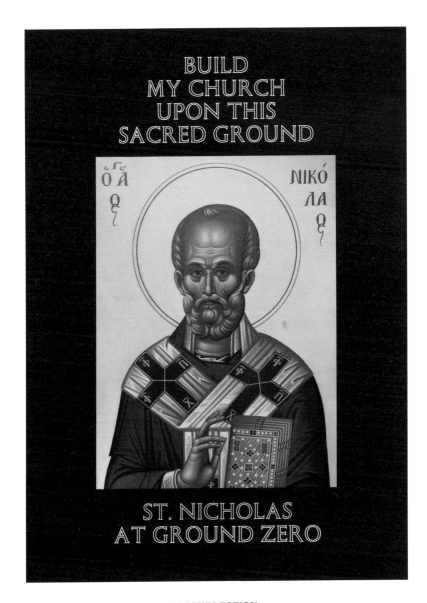

BUILD
MY CHURCH
UPON THIS
SACRED GROUND

ST. NICHOLAS
AT GROUND ZERO

RESURRECTION

On the tragic day of September 11, 2001, the Saint Nicholas Greek Orthodox Church was erased
from the face of the earth when the World Trade Center collapsed on it.
The beautiful new church designed by Santiago Calatrava, who drew inspiration from the iconic
Hagia Sophia in Istanbul, Turkey, should be completed in time
for its 100th anniversary in 2016. It will include a memorial park, a place of meditation
for people of all denominations, and be gloriously dedicated to
the 2,753 innocent lives lost that day.

LEAAATHER

UNBELIEVABLE LEATHER THAT STRETCHES WITH THE BODY! SUPPLE, COMFORTABLE, LUXURIOUS.

TYPE TALKS!

A perfect example of a functional brand name, visually imparting information in a nanosecond. Yeaaah for stretchable leather.

LOIS/USA

LOIS OF THE BRONX?

The names of the ad agencies I founded were Papert Koenig Lois (1960-1967), Lois Holland Callaway (1967-1975), and Lois, Pitts, Gershon (1978-1995). When Bill Pitts and Dick Gershon retired in the mid-1990s, in the style of André Joseph Marie, who had brazenly labeled himself Charles de Gaulle (and to reflect our added offices in Chicago, Houston and L.A.) I re-branded my agency Lois/USA. (I toyed with the name Lois of the Bronx, but it didn't seem to have quite the ring as Charles of France.)

**FOR THE PIONEERING
LITTLE RED SCHOOLHOUSE**

in Greenwich Village,
a symbol of kids from kindergarten
to the 12th grade —
from child to confident youth.
(And in the racist days of
the early '60s, the
logo proudly courted
African-Americans.)

FOR A HARD-TO-FIND RESTAURANT

We named this restaurant
tucked away
in the CBS building
after its location,
Ground Floor Cafe,
and turned
the logo into a discreet
exterior direction
sign so as not to insult
the understated
mood of the great
Eero Saarinen edifice.

A BRAND
CREATED BY RESEARCH
(KIND OF)

In 1964, Quaker Oats refused my
insistence that marketing a syrup was a
no-brainer. Until my cunning research,
where 88 out of 100 women insisted that
non-existent Aunt Jemima Syrup was
their "favorite syrup"! So Quaker poured
it on, and our ad campaign,
Aunt Jemima, what took you so long?...
made them No. 1 in no time.

LE TOUT LOGO

A logo with a French hand-scripted
touch that re-launched Manhattan's most
romantic West Side spot.

AN ORGIASTIC PROMISE OF FOOD, DRINK, AND CULTURAL NOSTALGIA

When Graydon Carter acquired The Waverly Inn, he commissioned Edward Sorel to create murals throughout the restaurant depicting the culture gods that hung out there during the heyday of the legendary Greenwich Village hot spot. So I thought it was befitting that their logo should be a concept drawn by Sorel. We conspired to depict an ancient god of Western Civilization by rendering a Maenad in ecstasy "a woman who participates in orgiastic Dionysian rites," servicing Dionysus, the God of Wine and of Pleasures, in the supreme style of 5th century BC Greek vase painting. Carter, the superb editor of *Vanity Fair* for over 20 years, obviously considered our logo too titillating, and rejected it.

THOU SHALT GO TO OMGFAST FOR THE FASTEST HOME INTERNET IN FLORIDA

Enlisting Michelangelo's depiction of God from the ceiling of the Sistine Chapel came in handy for the imagery of a hi-speed internet service named OMGFAST.

IF YOU CAN'T CHANGE THEIR LOGO, TELL THEM TO GO TO ELLE.

Go to Elle was my naughty way to get plenty of attention for the exciting fashion magazine, and for the full year they ran with it, their circulation increased and they boosted their ad pages a heavenly 12%. But, after a critical article in the trade press, the French honcho at Hachette Filipacchi chickened out. The devil made him do it.

"MM-MM-GOOD"

A witty, surprising, conceptual graphic solution (and discovery) of the letter formation, look and sound of the name "Jimmy Kimmel."

CELEBRITY TRANSFORMED INTO *$ELLEBRITY*

My 2003 book on the art of choosing celebrities to sell a product featured over 400 case studies where I proved that celebrity, used creatively, was transformed into *$ellebrity*. Let's face it, it's a starstruck world. We're all suckers for a famous face.

THE PICASSO PEACENIK LOGO

There was no high quality cosmetically-oriented, feminine soap available in America's supermarkets until Dove. In 1972, during the Cold War, any visual of a dove was considered a "Picasso peacenik" symbol. But sanity prevailed at corporate headquarters. Years later Unilever couldn't keep their mitts off it and the package design lost its flair...but the Dove flies on.

THE BALLSIEST ACTIVE SPORTSWEAR IN THE WORLD

The extroverted Serbian, Novak Djokovic, one of the greatest tennis players of all time, didn't have the balls to run with this logo.

by Novak Djokovic

MY CRAPPY LOGO

Las Vegas casinos needed a logo for OZNO, a new 3-dice craps game. With the fee for this logo, I bought my baby a new pair of (Blahnik) shoes.

America's Independent Wildcatters

BUT WE'RE STILL DEPENDENT ON FOREIGN OIL

In 1965, a logo of a helmeted wildcat for America's Independent Wildcatters, a maverick organization of oil drillers seeking fewer government sanctions in their quest for new oil fields in America. The burning question back then was: *Are we going to beg the Persian Gulf states for it… or are we going to drill our own!*

AM I PROUD OF THIS LOGO? HELL, YES!

In 1989, the AFL-CIO needed a populist, power logo to halt their decreasing power of influence in fighting for the respect of American workers. Did I have trouble coming up with a punchy slogan? Hell, No! I created the ringing cry, *Union, Yes!* Am I proud of helping the labor movement in America? Hell, Yes!

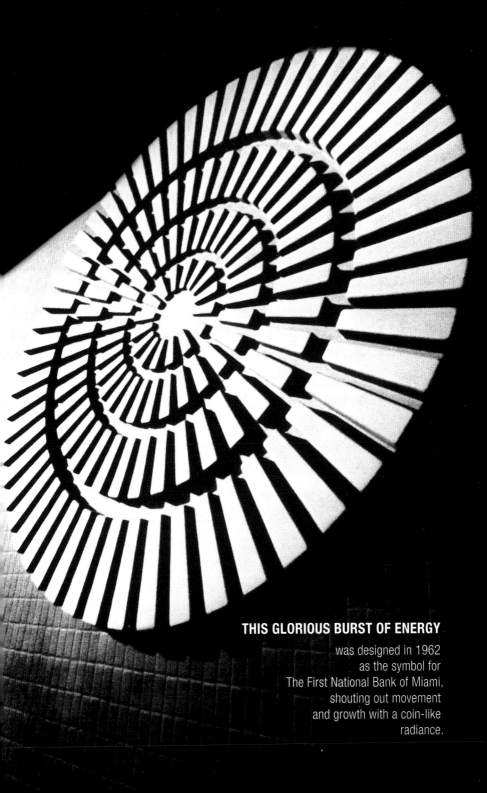

THIS GLORIOUS BURST OF ENERGY
was designed in 1962
as the symbol for
The First National Bank of Miami,
shouting out movement
and growth with a coin-like
radiance.

A WINDSWEPT LOGO

For a new restaurant at Lambert Field in St. Louis,
The Hangar, decorated with artifacts
of the early days of aviation, a swooping, high-flying
logo promises friendliness and coziness in
an age of cold turkey jetport restaurants—and maybe
even an extra helping of romance.

"Our people are pros, just like us."

MantleMen&NamathGirls

A BRAND NAME STARRING THE TWO SEXIEST MEN IN AMERICA

In 1968, my ad agency, Lois Holland Callaway, partnered up with
Mickey Mantle and Joe Namath to create a super-sized employment agency.
The logo was a cinch. (How do you beat the image of two of the
greatest superstars, ever!) Mantle Men & Namath Girls was the biggest employment
agency in the Metropolitan area for two years, but we fell victim to Nixon's
first recession and Mickey, Joe, Ron Holland, Jim Callaway and I all lost our jobs!

A BRAND NAME SPOKEN AT EVERY WEDDING CEREMONY

We are gathered here today
to brand these Wedding Planners
in just two words:

"I DO"

MY TWO-BIT LOGO

In 1967 Stevens couldn't sell Spirit hosiery for 50¢ a pair because women perceived them as being cheaply made. So I re-packaged them with the outrageous name 25¢ a leg and an ad campaign that declared *Anyone who pays more ought to have her knees examined!* For four years (until they had to increase the price) 25¢ a leg walked off department store shelves.

EVERY GREAT LOGO MAKES A SPLASH

But this one, for a donut and coffee joint,
goes way overboard. My name and visual is a SlamDunk.

THE LOGO THAT INSPIRED BIG-MOUTH TV JOURNALISM (SHAME ON ME)

Bob Pittman asked me to choose a screwball radio personality
to front a popular-appeal TV talk show.
One look at Morton Downey Jr's choppers and I knew he was
our man. My "Mighty Mouth" logo became the
symbol of the birth of no-holds barred TV journalism in America.

A TART PSEUDO-LOGO

In my book, *Iconic America*,
I created a pseudo-logotype of the
most spectacular failure
in the history of the American
auto industry (before the
economic crash of GM in 2009).
My acidic image makes the
name Edsel synonymous with
the proverbial "lemon."

NEW YORK, NEW YORK,

A CITY SO GREAT THEY NAMED IT TWICE

THE NAME & LOGO THAT LAUNCHED CITY MAGAZINES IN THE U.S.

Until *New York*, no "city" magazine existed. Originally created by my art staff and me in 1962 as a Sunday supplement for *The New York Herald Tribune*, it then evolved into *New York* in 1968, a weekly that still flourishes, 47 years later.

THANK YOU, JOHNNY CARSON

We ran our TV campaign on NBC's *The Tonight Show* with Johnny Carson, hoping he would work our slogan over before and after each TV spot ran (including nights we weren't on). He did, and women ran to Bloomingdale's to look for this hangtag and stroke Highlander Suede coats.

Highlander Suede (for the 2nd best feeling in the world!)

GEN 2

PEACEMAKERS

THE SONS AND DAUGHTERS OF THE GREATEST PEACEMAKERS OF THE 20TH CENTURY,

Martin Luther King Jr., Mahatma Gandhi, Robert F. Kennedy, César Chávez, King Hussein of Jordan, Archbishop Desmond Tutu, Yitzhak Rabin, Pierre Trudeau and Rafik Harriri, form the nucleus of this organization dedicated to bringing peace to the world. The "V" sign serves as a double entendre action symbol for "peace" as well as "second generation."

"BUT LOIS, WILL ANYONE KNOW IT'S A RESTAURANT?

When I presented this acronym and logotype to the Runyonesque brothers,
Irving and Murray Riese, the legendary Manhattan restaurateurs,
Irving quietly asked if anyone would know if it was a restaurant! Murray snapped back:
"Irving...Beer, Onions, Steak, Salad! What are we selling?
SHOES?!"

CLASSIC
DANISH BEAUTY

An elegant Dansk
logo and
structural packaging
in the '60s
that contained the
now-classic,
iconic housewares
from Denmark.

GET IT?
The eyes of Cincinnati!

Wiii TV 64
THE EYES OF
CiNCiNNATi

AND THAT'S NO BULL

My name
and package design
for a Tequila
with a macho kick.
One golden shot
and you'll snort fire, gringo!

HOW'S THIS
FOR THE NAME OF AN OIL?

Could you think of a better
name than Slip to imply lubrication?
In 1962, the simple, startling
graphics of this motor additive was a
standout on gas station shelves.

Shears atSears

A CUTTING EDGE logo for a chain of beauty parlors at Sears stores.

A LOGO THAT PORTRAYS THE HUNGRY, BIG-MOUTH COLLEGE STUDENT

We were going up against Mory's (from the *Whiffenpoof Song*), the most famous college restaurant in the world. Hungry Charley's became this hunger-crazed character with a cavernous mouth. When the take-out box opens, the mouth gets bigger and bigger and bigger.

WE NAMED HIM CHARLEY O

We designed his signature.
We decorated his walls.
And we dropped in for a few
pops every week to bask
in his success.

"Solid drink
and good food.
That's my theory."

A HALE & HEARTY LOGO

for a New York Metropolitan area
soup, salad and sandwich
restaurant chain that was rejected.
(You can't win'em all.
Compare it to the logo they use now
and it'll break your heart.)

WHAT'S UP AT UPI?

With this dramatic new logo
and aggressive theme,
One up on the World,
this formidable news agency,
established in 1907,
told the media world they
were back in action.

Where you meet Your Other Face!

TOURNEAU TIMEMACHINE

TOURNEAU TIMEMACHINE, NAMED FOR A SUPERSTORE OF WATCHES

In 1997, on superactive 57th Street, my name TOURNEAU TIMEMACHINE futuristically described the dazzling modernity of our time, and my ultimate status slogan, *Where you meet Your Other Face*, added the mystery, and double entendre, of time travel.

THE FIRST FAX MACHINE

Prior to the introduction of the ubiquitous facsimile machine was the Exxon Qwip in the mid-1970s, and American big business went *Qwip qwazy*. But Exxon failed to keep up in the early 1980's when the technology went digital.

WHAT'S MORE ROMANTIC THAN THE MOON?

Cafe Galleria, in Canada, wanted to capture the new night life market of Montreal. The phases of the moon suggest nighttime and, of course, the romance of couples coming together.

A NAME AND LOGO FOR PAY-PER-VIEW SUPERFIGHTS ON TV? HOW ABOUT TVKO!

When Time and Warner merged, I branded their enormously profitable HBO championship fights with this knockout name. Their very first event, *The Battle of the Ages*, between George Foreman and Evander Holyfield, had a record-breaking pay-per-view of $60 million.

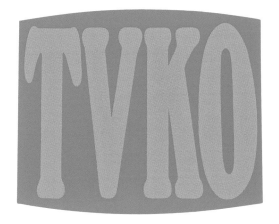

PARADE Of Stars
An Actors Fund Benefit at the Palace

DIRECTORS LOVE
TO SEE THEIR NAMES IN LIGHTS

A logo featuring Billy Hudson and his superstar film production company, who always directed boffo TV commercials.

MY SMALL CONTRIBUTION
FOR THE DAUGHTER OF A 9/11 VICTIM

When my great pal, former N.Y. Giants football great Dick Lynch, lost his son in the 9/11 attacks, he formed the The Richard Lynch Memorial Fund to benefit Olivia, his beloved granddaughter (daddy's little girl).

A DANCING LOGO

A headless, strutting, Old Gold cigarette pack sporting great gams from an early '50s TV variety show inspired this Parade of Stars logo (repeated 12 times in an accordion-fold chorus line for the mailing of an invitation).

TO BECOME A SENATOR FROM THE STATE OF NEW YORK, I CONVINCED ROBERT KENNEDY TO "ADMIT" HE WAS A CARPETBAGGER

In 1964, less than two years after President John F. Kennedy was assassinated, Robert, his "ruthless little brother," ran for the Senate. Working for him, he struck me as an honest, principled leader who was desperately needed by New York (even if RFK wasn't a New Yorker). I knew he had to sweep the "carpetbagger" label or his candidacy could be stillborn. So in the early summer, months before any political advertising blitz normally began in those days, I convinced Bobby and Steve Smith (his brother-in-law and campaign manager) to let me plaster New York State with the straightforward message, *Let's put Bobby Kennedy to work for New York*, branding him as a man who had ties in the nation's capitol and would kick ass to help the citizens of New York. Almost overnight, this disarmingly honest strategy paid off as the "carpetbagger" handle evaporated. Robert Kennedy won the senatorial race with a plurality of 720,000 votes. Those early posters helped him totally ignore the carpetbagger stigma, and he spoke to the voters of New York state openly, honestly, and much of the time, inspirationally.

BOBBY NEVER FORGAVE ME

As the campaign for the senate entered the last month, I feared that Robert Kennedy could lose to incumbent Kenneth Keating, as a result of a large undecided bloc of democrats troubled by Bobby's unfortunate stint when he was a young man working with the red-baiting Roy Cohn. I begged Kennedy and Steve Smith to let me brand all the remaining commercials I was producing with the line, *Get on the Johnson, Humphrey, Kennedy team*. Bobby was stunned at my suggestion, because he truly hated Lyndon Johnson (I mean *hated*). I argued LBJ and HHH were sure to get most democratic votes in the state – so we had to convince New Yorkers that when they entered the voting booth, they must vote the straight democrat party line! After a few furious arguments, Kennedy bit his lip and through gritted teeth muttered, "Do it." When he finally won with a gigantic plurality, he was pissed that I had convinced him to associate his name in any way with the likes of Lyndon Baines Johnson. At his election night victory party, Senator Kennedy gave me the cold shoulder. But I forgave him...

LET'S PUT BOBBY KENNEDY TO WORK FOR NEW YORK

MY MR. BIG IDEA LOGO

The advertising world has known me as "Mr. Big Idea" since the early '60s. In 1991, I designed this book cover logotype for *What's the Big Idea?*, basically a teaching course on how to create fresh,

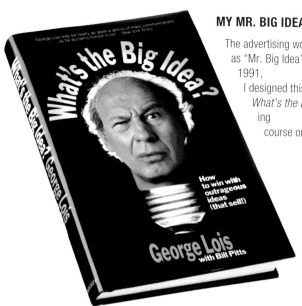

MY NAME FOR A BEAUTY PRODUCT FOR A SHIT-KICKING JEANS BRAND

A jeans brand named after Route 66, America's iconic, down-home highway, inexplicably wanted to sell a line extension of *beauty* products. Absurd – but creativity overcomes everything. I recommended a line of hair products and I named them...*Root 66*!

A LOGO THAT AIMS FOR THE STARS

For Seth Abraham, who, as the kingpin of HBO Sports, consistently brought titanic boxing events to the cable world, a logo for his fledgling sports consulting enterprise, where he always aims for the stars.

THESE TWIN BOXES,

placed together to complete the beautiful face, acted as an eye-popping logotype for Finesse stockings in store windows and shelves all over America. (I was sent dozens of Polaroid's of store windows showing only displays of this ordinarily low-interest item.)

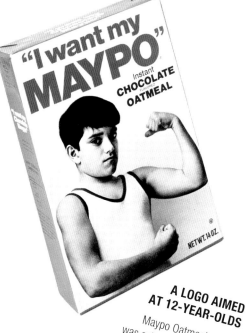

A LOGO AIMED AT 12-YEAR-OLDS

Maypo Oatmeal Cereal was selling, but only to the 3- to 6-year-old market. So I created a TV campaign to sell to kids up to the age of 12, depicting the greatest professional athletes of the day, actually crying "I want my Maypo!" The campaign was so successful, I filled the supermarket shelves with images of healthy youngsters. (The superboy on this package was my son Harry, age 10.)

LIGHTING UP THE TV SPORTS WORLD

With the merger of Time and Warner in 1990,
Seth Abraham founded Time Warner Sports. Before the ink on the agreement dried,
I created this scoreboard-like animated TV logo.

A SURPRISING
TOUCH OF FRUIT JUICE

inspired this name for
a flavored bottled water from PepsiCo.

EVERYBODY LOVES A GOOSE

A group of twenty-something entrepreneurs
approached me with their concept for a website
that would attract young go-getters looking
for info and tips on their road to success.
So I created a website name that
declared "if you're in your twenties,
its time to stick your neck out
and getagoose."

A SMOKIN' LOGO

My logo portrays two royal Indonesian masks – representing two brand names – proudly flaunting cigars that sprang from their exotic lands, firmly clenched in their rapturous smiles.

INDONESIAN TOBACCO CO.

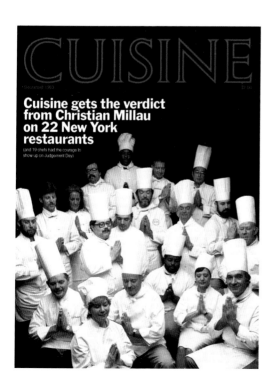

CUISINE

Cuisine gets the verdict from Christian Millau on 22 New York restaurants

(and 19 chefs had the courage to show up on Judgement Day)

BUSINESS AT CUISINE WAS AS FLAT AS A PANCAKE

So in 1983-84, I did a complete redesign, starting with the logo and creating six of their covers. *Cuisine* was transformed from a loser to a winner! Frightened by *Cuisine's* soaring circulation and hot ad sales, Condé Nast honcho Sy Newhouse bought *Cuisine* for big bucks to keep readers and advertisers from comparing *Gourmet*, his lackluster food publication, to the new *Cuisine*. He then folded the exciting, new *Cuisine* in an attempt to pick up their readers. "If you can't beat'em, buy'em."

THE NAUGA MAY BE UGLY,
BUT HIS VINYL HIDE IS BEAUTIFUL

There were dozens of vinyl copycats on the market, all indistinguishable
(at least in the consumers mind). So to separate
Naugahyde from the others, I created The Nauga, the mythical beast
who contributes his hide for Naugahyde. The beast was a
logo and also a spokesman for Naugahyde on TV, a seven-foot costume that
nearly suffocated the comedian Chuck McCann inside.
The Nauga also became a highly visible
tag that hung on every Naugahyde product.
And finally, he became
the 12-inch doll you see here,
one of the most
popular premiums ever.

CHEW ON THIS!

An award given by the Distinguished Restaurants of North America. Tom Margittai (co-owner of The Four Seasons) and I created the acronym DiRoNA, derived from the five words of their organization, and sculpted a gourmet sublimely munching his meal. The spiffy stainless steel DiRoNA proudly hangs in 300 restaurants throughout the U.S., Canada and Mexico.

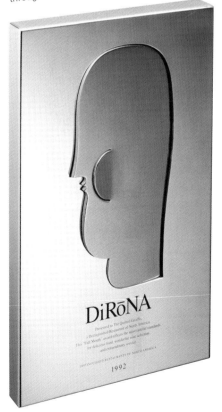

I BRANDED THE FIRST WHITE TEA... WHITE T

White tea buds plucked from the very top of the white tea plant offer up to five times more antioxidants than green tea (antioxidants help fight cancer and osteoporosis). So I simply called the drink White T, with a booming capital T.

BRANDING A LABOR UNION
BORN WITH BLOOD, SWEAT AND TEARS

Before the International Ladies Garment Workers Union, there were
sweatshops. In the early 20th century,
New York was filled with immigrants, working in wretched conditions,
barely eking out a living. Hard-won unionism
had allowed thousands of members of the ILGWU to work in dignity and
make ends meet. In 1959, I branded their union
with the symbol of freedom, the welcoming Statue of Liberty
bearing the torch of liberty – and a child holding up an
ice cream cone to symbolize the new land's promised benefits of freedom:
food, shelter and security for the hard working
women of America. The synergy of the images served as a logotype
for the ILGWU for almost three decades.

ILGWU

INTERNATIONAL
LADIES GARMENT
WORKERS
UNION

JOIN THE NEW YORK BETS

In 1972, I initiated every
New Yorker into a new team:
You're too heavy for the Mets?
You're too light for the Jets?
You're too short for the Nets?
You're just right for the Bets!
My "clean" sports angle
made Off-Track Betting socially okay,
New Yorkers entered sleazy,
smoke-filled OTB parlors in droves,
and the city made a bundle.

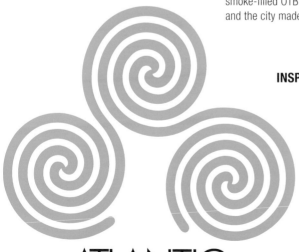

INSPIRED BY PRE-HISTORIC
GREEK ART

With shipping interests in
Greece, my design for
Atlantic Bank incorporates
circles in a continuous
spiral of undulating rhythm,
strongly reminiscent
of ancient Cycladic and
Minoan designs,
with a powerful graphic
resemblance to
the movement of the sea.

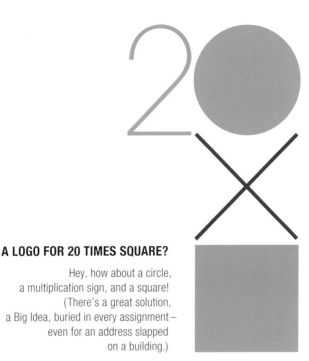

A LOGO FOR 20 TIMES SQUARE?

Hey, how about a circle,
a multiplication sign, and a square!
(There's a great solution,
a Big Idea, buried in every assignment –
even for an address slapped
on a building.)

MY HOMAGÉ TO THE MOTHER GODDESS

One of the great museums of the world, The Goulandris Museum of Cycladic Art
in Athens, needed a name and logo for a society of backers. So I named it
Cycladic Lovers, and showed one of their prehistoric Mother Goddesses (3,000 BC)
as they were discovered, lying on their backs as companions for the afterlife,
exerting supreme power.

CYCLADIC

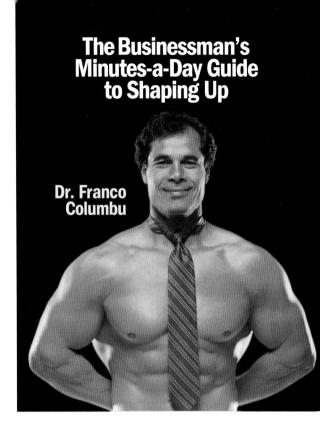

The Businessman's Minutes-a-Day Guide to Shaping Up

Dr. Franco Columbu

EXERCISE FOR MEN IN SUITS

As successful as Franco Columbu had been as a world famous body builder (prominent in the training of Arnold Schwarzenegger and twice a Mr. Olympia champion himself) his career as a Doctor of Chiropractic, and as a consultant to sports teams and Hollywood stars has made him a living legend in the world of Sports Medicine and Kinesiology. His book teaching business people to actually exercise during the work day is a classic.

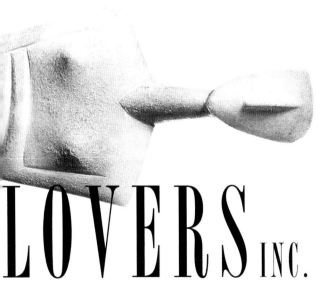

LOVERS INC.

A LOGO AS A DIRECTIONAL SIGN

In 1982, I designed an "action logo,"
a circular J in the form of a
directional sign, which almost forced
you to make a turn into a
Jiffy Lube station. The pioneering
company quickly changed
the way America changed its oil!

YOUWANNA LOGO?

For an internet video search engine,
along came the bigwanna, auditioning to be the
google of the Video Age.

THANK YOU, JERRY SEINFELD

YadaYada.com would have been the first internet
search engine for PDA's where you could surf the web and
yada yada yada to your hearts content –
but they got blown out of the water when the .com
bubble burst in the year 2000.

THE GREAT CARUSO

An iconic name for an Italian prosecco, displaying a beautiful
self-portrait by the pioneer of recorded music,
the great Italian tenor Enrico Caruso. It was drawn in 1902,
the year his recording of *Pagliacci*
was the first record to sell one million copies.

KEEPING THE WILLIWEAR BRAND ALIVE

WilliWear was the creation of fashion designer
Willi Smith. In 1976, he founded a youthful, dynamic clothing line
that took the country by storm. In 1987, as his
company was continuing to flourish, he died at the age of 39,
succumbing to AIDS. In 1995, a new group took
over his foundering brand to resuscitate his name and keep
his legacy alive. I redesigned their logo, with the
two never-ending I's, running into infinity – and the brand
lives on, and on.

WILLI SMITH

WilliWear

IN BELOVED REMEMBRANCE

On September 21, 1978, 16 days after my son Harry's 20th birthday,
he was struck down with an undetected heart disorder, long-QT syndrome, which can
kill young people by disrupting their heartbeat. Harry Joe was a powerfully
strong young man, a living incarnation of the great Herakles, a three-letter athlete,
a legendary warrior on the football field for the McBurney School in Manhattan
(and at the time of his death, the head of TV production at my ad agency). In 1987, the
newly relocated McBurney school dedicated the Harry Lois Memorial Gymnasium
in my son's honor, and I branded the signage with an image that echoes the ancient gold
and silver Herakles coins (which actually portrayed the profile
of the Alexander the Great).

1958-1978

THE HARRY LOIS
MEMORIAL GYMNASIUM
JANUARY 23, 1987

A GOOD LOGO
NEEDS TO BE ON TARGET!

In 2004, Leslee Dart, a hotshot PR star,
was founding a new company
and needed a new name and logo.
A no-brainer if there ever
was one: I would call it The Dart Group
(a perfect double entendre)
and the logo would represent their
movies, marketing and media
target – with a red bullseye. She didn't
go for the name and she didn't
go for the target. Go figure.

THE DART GROUP

BUSINESS IS A WAR GAME

In the year 2K, Opcenter was pioneering
the necessity of ahead-of-the-art strategic thinking
and implementation to help companies
achieve systems and infrastructure, for success in the
revolutionary new world of Ecommerce.

OPCE
Positioning for Attack in

AH VITE KVEEN!

When I showed the Russian chess champion Garry Kasparov my poster for the 1990 World Chess Championship in Manhattan, the white chess piece between his profile and Anatoly Karpov's hit him like an emotional illumination, and he gasped in astonishment and proclaimed, "*Na Zdorovye, tovarich! Kasparov and Karpov, nose-to-nose, and betveen them— ah vite kveen!*"

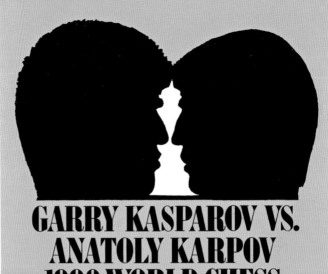

GARRY KASPAROV VS. ANATOLY KARPOV 1990 WORLD CHESS CHAMPIONSHIP

OCTOBER 8 – NOVEMBER 10, 1990 NEW YORK CITY

NTER

the age of the Internet!

MY ANTI-SLOGAN

My first book repeats the well-meaning but suffocating advice given to me by my mother, father, sisters, teachers, coaches, sergeants, lawyers, colleagues and clients during my long career in the ad business: *George, be careful*, symbolized on my book cover by the fearful hand of Michelangelo's God warning me to tread lightly. (I continue to reject all their advice, and my 1972 book cover remains my anti-logo.)

George, be careful

A Greek florist's kid in the roughhouse world of advertising

George Lois with Bill Pitts

FOR A HIP CLOTHING BRAND

In 1999, this hip clothing brand would have made hipO the king of the internet jungle for selling activewear online. But the entrepreneur from India "didn't get it" (and I'm not lion).

hip

hipO.com

SPA CUISINE

THE MOST RIPPED-OFF BRAND NAME EVER

Until Spa Cuisine, in 1980, conventional wisdom dictated that a four-star dining experience and good nutrition were incompatible. Spa Cuisine at The Four Seasons restaurant instantly attracted thousands of devotees and imitators all over the world, making my brand name generic for diet gourmet food. (We had a legal right to sue anyone in the world for ripping off our registered name, but we'd be in court five days a week.)

BRANDING TODAY'S USE OF THE ENGLISH LANGUAGE

A poster designed for the Wolfsonian Museum telling it like it is:
It's almost impossible to watch an hour of live TV without hearing intelligent people slaughter the English language. I mean, like, if you wrote the way millions of people talk these days, you'd be considered a dummy, y'know?

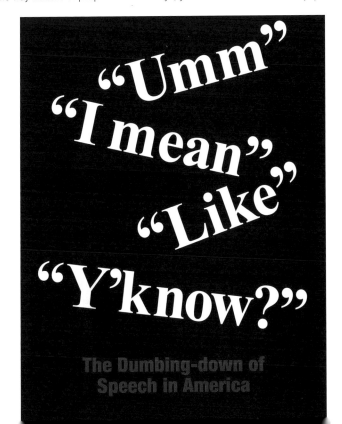

IM-PEACH!

THE BUSH ADMINISTRATION IS ROTTEN TO THE CORE!

PUSHING PEACHES

This was an unheeded call to impeach the President of the United States (sadly, the Democratic Party chickened out). My juicy Im-peach approach was conceived as a way to add style and wit to a deadly serious rebuke of a catastrophic presidency (and it would have sold a hell of a lot of Georgia peaches).

AN ICONIC BOOK TITLE

My *Iconic America* title and logotype wraps around my 2007 book, from sea to shining sea. (When you open the cover, you take a roller-coaster ride through the eye-popping panorama of American pop culture.)

Looming ahead of us,
a point beyond which there is no return, but

THERE IS STILL TIME!

Peter Seidel

A DEFINITIVE BOOK ON GLOBAL WARMING

With the rapid self-destruction of our environment,
our very survival is at stake. This 2015 book gives facts, details and
clear scientific overviews of global warming,
giving clear insight to the devastation being caused by the
procrastination of world leaders.
My book title and subhead says it all.

PAUL KOVI
STAR SEARCH
MEMORIAL SCHOLARSHIPS

IN HONOR OF MY GREAT FRIEND, PAUL KOVI

A logo for a Hospitality Management Baccalaureate of Technology degree program
at the New York City Technical College, in honor of Paul Kovi,
the consummate food impresario, and co-owner of The Four Seasons restaurant
from 1973 to 1995.

A MOVING LOGO

In a most un-British location, Florida,
this immediately identifiable
bus delivered what it promised: bountiful
gourmet beef dinners and beer.
(And the toy double-decker bus the
restaurant gave to each diner
were always a hit.)

TWO LOGOS TURNED DOWN
BY A CRABBY CLIENT

This memorable logo for a new
Mexican restaurant on East 19th street that
showcased a ravenous monkey
knocking down a margarita and taco was rejected,
alas, by a client who was no swinger.

The same client turned down my oxymoron
logo of a happy crab
for a seafood dive next door to Chango.

THE TIFFANY OF ICE CREAM PARLORS
NEEDED A NAME AND A FACE

In 1971, Mr. Jennings, a prankster soda chef
who drew adoring fans at Hick's,
a venerable fruiterer, defected after 26 years
to open his idea of a dream ice cream
parlor, at 28 East 70th St. One look at his puss
and his unique soda creations that
resembled Louis Comfort Tiffany glass, inspired
me to name his parlor Old Fashioned
Mr. Jennings. In our promotional copy we spoke
of his homey philosophy: "First God
created heaven and earth. Then He created
soda fountains. And that is how it
should be. Don't let the devil fill your mind with
thoughts of calories. Always be polite
to Mr. Jennings. He'll keep us young forever.
He doesn't care for war, he doesn't
care for jewels, he doesn't care for architecture.
Mr. Jennings knows what counts. Sodas.
And heavenly sweets. Blasphemous blendings
of delectable fruits. No matter how
many years you live, everything in Mr. Jennings'
place tastes as good as treats did when
you were a kid. Guaranteed."

FEAR ENDS.

DENNIS KUCINICH FOR PRESIDENT

HOPE BEGINS.

A LOGO FOR A POLITICIAN WHO WAS RIGHT ABOUT EVERYTHING

In the 2004 Democratic presidential primaries, Representative Dennis Kucinich was the only candidate who voted against an out-of-control Bush administration that clearly intended to attack Saddam Hussein with an illegal war on Iraq. Kucinich was right when he doubted the existence of weapons of mass destruction; was right that the administration, in the name of fighting terrorism, would bring about the destruction of our civil liberties; was right that we were creating a world of new terrorists with our illegal actions; and absolutely right that we would lose the love and respect of the whole world. Even though he had no chance to win the nomination, I was proud to help bring Kucinich's warnings to America, but it fell on deaf ears.

MY FIRST CONCEPTUAL LOGO (AT AGE 9)

Recently, while digging through a box of childhood belongings, I came upon a book of stories from Greek mythology, printed in Greek, marked throughout in 1941 as part of my mandatory Greek lessons. Along with my markings were cartoon drawings of Hitler, Hirohito, and Mussolini, the Fascist follower of Hitler who had invaded Greece in 1940. Below the caricatures, I had drawn my first conceptual logo: a swastika in the center of the Japanese flag of the Rising Sun, forming a symbol for the despotic Axis powers.

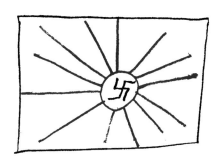

THE MOVEABLE LOGO

In 1972, as the newly elected president of the New York Art Directors Club, I founded their long overdue Hall of Fame. Teaming up with the great graphic designer Gene Federico (whose work had inspired me since I was a student at the High School of Music & Art) we designed a moveable, silky-silver A and D that elegantly fit together to form the most coveted lifetime achievement award in the world of graphic design.

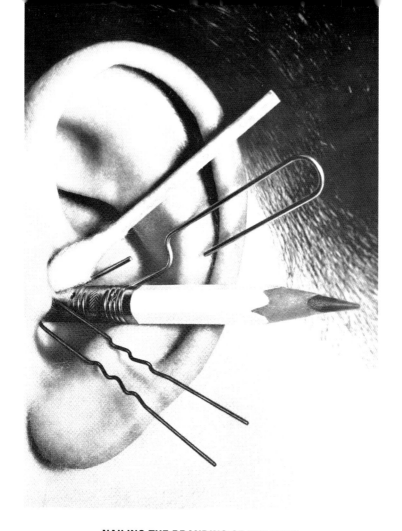

NAILING THE BRANDING OF THE NEED
FOR KERID EARDROPS WITH A BARBARIC IMAGE

In 1959, when I was a 27-year-old rookie art director at Doyle Dane Bernbach,
my first assignment was to create a campaign for a new product,
Kerid Eardrops. Burrowing through Kerid's research, I confirmed that most people
clean their ears poking around with pencils and bobby pins. I pushed
that finding to its graphic brink by showing this colossal close-up of an ear being
nailed by a pencil, a paperclip, and assorted hardware. The ad screamed:
Don't risk a punctured eardrum by poking and stabbing your ears – use Kerid eardrops.
Outraged veteran creative people at DDB formed a posse and galloped
up to Bill Bernbach's office to protest my "disgusting" campaign. Bill Bernbach
patted them on the head and herded them out the door, because
he understood that there is imagery that shocks people for shock's sake – and
imagery that attracts and holds attention because of a
meaningful and memorable message.

Lubalin DORFSMAN LOIS INC.

MY DREAM TEAM AGENCY

In 1958, the graphic pioneer Herb Lubalin and I schemed to leave
Sudler & Hennessy, a pharmaceutical ad agency where Herb was the head of creative,
and I was his consumer art director. We, along with CBS Television
Creative Chief Lou Dorfsman, planned to open what would have been the second
creative ad agency in the world (after Doyle Dane Bernbach).
But Lou chickened out, and we canned the project. All that remains is this co-designed logo.
I went on, in 1960, to open Papert Koenig Lois, and my dream
of founding "the second creative agency" came true.

A BUDDING LOGO for a non-profit community task force
that promotes Northeast Ohio's local food products.

Media Peop**é**le

BRANDING MY MoMA SHOW

In 2008, the Museum of Modern Art opened a yearlong
exhibition honoring the installation in their
permanent collections of the *Esquire* covers created by me
from 1961 to 1972. This book, with my
personal recollections, acts as a definitive record of a decade
of covers that MoMA called "iconic images
and a visual timeline of the turbulent events of the 1960s."

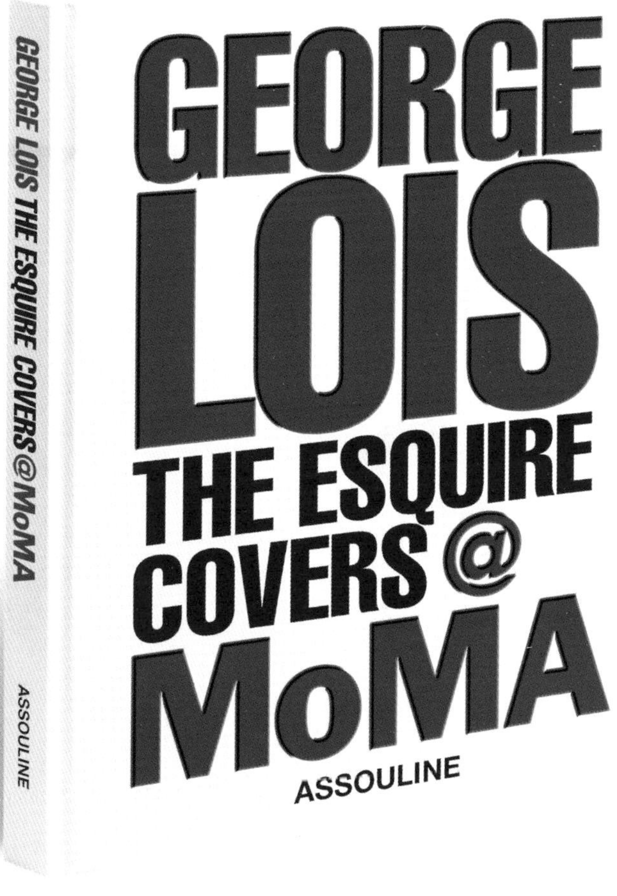

GEORGE LOIS THE ESQUIRE COVERS @MoMA

ASSOULINE

GEORGE
LOIS
THE ESQUIRE
COVERS @
MoMA

ASSOULINE

A LOGO KILLED BY THE COMPUTER

Before the introduction of the
IBM typewriter that corrected typos,
a logo for the media guru,
Charlie Mandel, and his magazine
Media People, on the business
and monkey business of the media world.
With the advent of electronic
typewriters and the computer, my
¢ typo got erased.

OH-GEE

To me, this seemingly unpronounceable four letter name, Oggi (oh-gee),
called for an eccentric typeface to suggest the unique fare to be found in this superb gift shop.
The brand can be recognized a block away on every shopping bag and package.

THE MIKE DOUGLAS SHOW

SPEAK INTO THE MIKE

Mike Douglas, a popular daytime
TV talk show host in the
1960s and '70s, loved this logo
so much he actually started
to use an un-needed microphone
as a prop as he walked
among his adoring audience.

A DRAMATIC SYMBOL FOR ART & COPY

An award I designed in 1972 for the Art Directors Club (when I was their president)
and the Copy Club, when we joined forces for an
awards competition we named The One Show. This lucite, double-sided pencil
(that represented a combo of art and copy in one
blockbuster event) became the imagery of the show. The next year, The Copy Club added
art directors to their Hall of Fame, changed their name
to The *One* Club, and appropriated the two-sided pencil concept as a logo
for their very successful creative club.

THE ONE SHOW

THE ART DIRECTORS CLUB
THE COPY CLUB OF NEW YORK

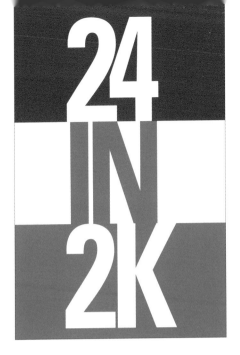

A LOGO THAT HUNG FROM THE RAFTERS

In the year 2K, I designed a special logo for banners, buttons, bus posters, cufflinks, etc., for a "Legends and Champions Tribute to Bill Bradley for President," fundraiser in his quest for the Democratic nomination. The banners surrounded Bradley's retired No. 24 jersey that gloriously hangs from the rafters of Madison Square Garden.

STAR BUCKS PR

FOR A PR COMPANY REPRESENTING MONEY-MAKING STARS

This name and logo was turned down by a prestigious company – I'd give you the name they finally chose, but you, like the rest of the world, probably never heard of them. (But if they had bought this logo, their name would be on everyone's lips whenever they sipped a cup of coffee.)

THE ALL POWERFUL ZEUS

DEI (The Public Power Corporation of Greece)
is the biggest electric power company in Greece,
controlled to an extent by the government,
producing and supplying electricity to the whole nation.
The image of Zeus, Greece's mythological
king of the gods, who was depicted in ancient times
as overseeing the universe, is modernized
with today's accepted visual rendition of lightning,
as a metaphor for electrical power.

TWIN

TRANS-WORLD IDENTIFICATION NO.

NIML

**THE ONE-TWO PUNCH
ON & OFFLINE PROTECTION SYSTEM
AGAINST IDENTITY THEFT**

SEEING DOUBLE

Privacy, the internet and identity theft has become
a key issue in financial transactions.
Everyone has become afraid of Identity Theft.
Very afraid. But with a Twin account,
business affairs can be conducted securely,
on and off-line.

THE ART
OF AGGRESSIVE
SPORTS THERAPY

THE TRAINING CENTER
NEW YORK LOOKS UP TO

I emblazoned six gigantic U.S. Athletic Training Center
logos, at different angles, on the second story windows at
their location at Madison Avenue and 53rd Street,
powerfully beckoning Broadway dancers, ABT ballerinas,
major leaguers, Olympians and serious amateur
athletes. Gary Guerriero, Mary Leonard and Michelangelo's
iconic drawings of the human body have greeted
the gung-ho jocks at the door of USATC for over 20 years.

THE ABA LIVES
(AND DIES, AGAIN)

In the year 2000, I was part of
a hoop group that resurrected the legendary
American Basketball Association.
In the 1970s, with a fresh style of go-go ball,
they changed the rules, they changed
the game, and they even changed the basketball.
But even with the support of ex-ABA
greats like Dr. J, George Gervin, George McGinnis,
Connie Hawkins, and Rick Barry,
the moguls of the NBA played dirty,
and torpedoed us.

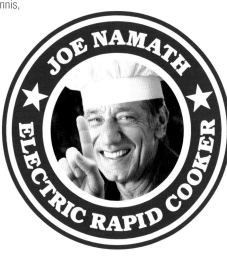

BROADWAY JOE GUARANTEES IT

Borrowing from my 1994
United States Athletic Training Center
logo (see previous page),
in 2014 I designed this logo for
Joe's super-heated stove,
specially created to function in
city dwellings, rivaling
the finest equipment at The Palm,
BLT Steak or Peter Lugar's.

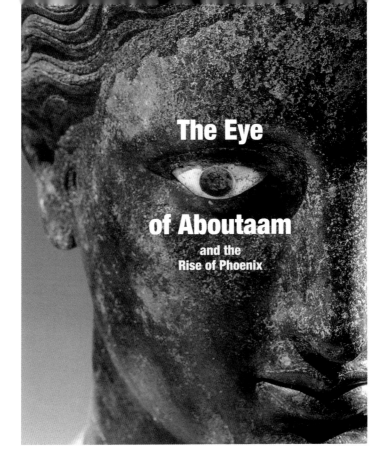

The Eye

of Aboutaam

and the
Rise of Phoenix

THE SHOCK OF THE OLD

Branding a book of some of the greatest masterworks of antiquities from the cultural hotspots
of western civilization, which have passed through the hands of the legendary
Aboutaam family. Phoenix Ancient Art, founded by the Lebanese Sleiman Aboutaam in 1968,
is now led by his sons Hicham and Ali, leading a new wave of dealers with
a soulful commitment to provenance and the rules of national ownership. (The cover depicts
Apollo the Python-Slayer, one of the finest classical Greek bronze statues ever created.)

A PALINDROME

is a word that reads the same way in either direction, coming
from the Greek word "running back again." The name
Xemex was coined by Steve Pappas, a Greek entrepreneur,
for his corporate name, so I emphasized
the palindrome with a backwards E. Come again?

ZOGR

IT'S GREEK TO ME

The Sigma Pharmaceutical Corporation wanted something modern, so I combined the Greek letters of their name, (Sigma-Phi) and melded them into a ligature. It suggests medical symbols, and appears strangely futuristic.

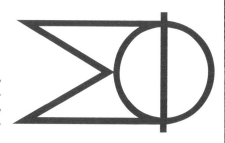

"THE CUSTOMERS ARE COMING, THE CUSTOMERS ARE COMING..."

The logo for Paul Revere's is a straightforward solution, but not as simplistic as it might seem. The moon reminds us of Revere's midnight ride, letting New York know this restaurant would be open late, and his slight leer suggests the action to be encountered at this successful bar and grill.

A GRIPPING LOGO

for an embracing harness that helps coordinate arm, hip and leg action during batting practice.

BASEBALL HIPGRIP TRAINER

APHOS

Let's talk it over at

SHAKE HANDS WITH THIS LOGO

For an authentic
English Ale & Chop House
deep in the lobby of the
then new Pan Am building,
I designed a friendly
symbol to attract those
harassed business commuters
who stream in and out
of Grand Central Station.
Ever get a warmer invitation?

BRANDING A MANHATTAN CORNER

In the mid-1980s, I named the Tourneau store
on the corner of Madison and 52nd street,
Tourneau Corner, describing the exact location
of the finest watch store in town.
(Mayor Koch of New York changed the existing
street signs to *Tourneau Corner!*)

TOURNEAU

52ND STREET

IKONIC!

Envirocare foresees the future with a revolutionary iKonoplastic flow-forming process to create a world of indestructible products of incredible strength and miraculous lightness.

IN THE EARLY YEARS OF THE AIDS EPIDEMIC

In 1989, a name and logo for the GHMC Benefit Concert at Radio City Music Hall. Arista's superstar musical talent performed through the night for the benefit of the Gay Men's Health Crisis.

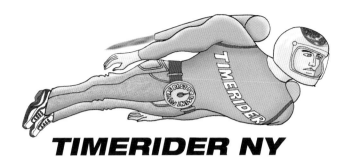

TIMERIDER NY

TIMERIDER TOURIST WELCOME CENTERS THROUGHOUT THE WORLD

Proposed welcome centers in New York, Los Angeles, Rome, Tokyo, etc. for people to view a 4•D film of a digital time ride through the past, present and future of the culture of each respective city, as well as real-time tourist information. Flames emit from two rockets strapped to the back of our TimeRider as he jets to historical points of destination by dialing a magical belt that he sets to enter the time period he desires. A thrilling ballad, *TimeRider in the Sky*, adapted from *Ghost Riders in the Sky*, by Johnny Cash, plays throughout.

MY EXID LOGO GETS THE DOOR

In 1992, for a new over-the-counter antacid, I proposed the name EXID (in the form of an exit sign). A major pharmaceutical company rejected it because they thought that every sighting of an exit sign in America would "immediately bring their new antacid to mind." "Of course it will," I bellowed, "that's the idea!" I politely burped, and exited their group grope meeting. (The name they finally chose was insipid, and their antacid bombed.)

THE WAVE OF THE FUTURE

Cargo and freight ships are some of the largest contributors to the pollution of the planet. New Wave is a revolutionary Hydrogen-on-Demand technology that supplements traditional oil fuel, dynamically increasing fuel economy and dramatically lowering planet-poisoning emissions.

I hang at

fash♥n
passi♥n

A PROPOSED WORLDWIDE FASHION NETWORK

A name and logo for a TV network to dramatically
present the fascinating, frivolous, inspiring, transforming and
passionate world of fashion, beauty and lifestyle.
It hasn't been produced yet, but this one could turn the fashion world on its head.

MY ANTI-PLAYBOY LOGO
(BANG! BANG! WE GOTCHA!)

In 1979, by outraunching *Playboy*, *Penthouse* hit
its all-time high of 4.7 million copies sold.
Bob Guccione asked me to flaunt his victory against
Hugh Hefner. When Hef saw my campaign,
headlined *Penthouse goes Rabbit Hunting*, he went
apoplectic, and threatened to sue The Gooch,
until he realized he was drawing nationwide attention
to the news that *Penthouse* was
overtaking *Playboy*.

ONE

TWO

THREE

In 1981, I had the honor to
design this book cover for Harold Hayes,
a decade after designing his
Esquire covers, many of which are now
in the permanent collections of the
Museum of Modern Art in New York. His
book, *Three Levels of Time*, was a
daring exploration of three intersecting
impulses: Instinct, Intelligence,
and Survival, weaving three intriguing
strands of narrative.

**THREE
LEVELS
OF TIME**

**THREE
LEVELS
OF TIME**

**THREE
LEVELS
OF TIME**

HAROLD T. P. HAYES

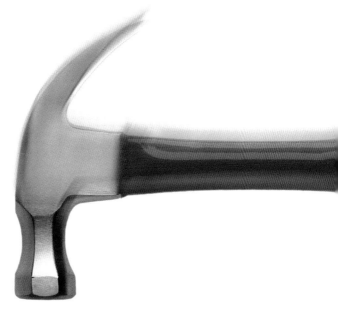

NAIL
YOUR
MORTGAGE

A GODSEND TO THE NEW HOME OWNERS OF AMERICA:
Nail Your Mortgage searches and nails down the most affordable,
transparent mortgage rate for your home, hammers out
all the negotiating with multiple banks (you're anonymous while
they're making the deal) and never charges a commission,
saving you thousands over all other mortgage brokers, only charging
a flat $750 fee the day you sign and receive
your pre-approved mortgage. Now *that's* a great deal.

The Bloody Nose

PROFESSIONAL FIGHTS UNDER THE BROOKLYN BRIDGE
AT THE SWANKIEST STEAKHOUSE IN TOWN

In 1964, Joe Baum, the legendary restaurant impresario, discovered an immense
stone-vaulted space under the spectacular Brooklyn Bridge – inspiring Joe and I to create a classy
steakhouse and hangout I named The Bloody Nose. A sensational bar, with hundreds
of banquettes surrounding a boxing ring, served by ex-fighters dolled up in tuxedos. Jake LaMotta
went on a weight-loss program to be one of our hosts, and we lined up Muhammad Ali
to train in our ring for some of his upcoming fights, surrounded by all the dining guys and dolls.
Mayor John Lindsay loved our project, seeing it as a ultra-sensational New York attraction.
Joe Baum worked out a deal with him, but just days before construction began, the weak-kneed
City Council bureaucrats (who had allowed the iconic Penn Station to be demolished
the year before) KO'ed The Bloody Nose because they claimed it
would have commercialized the legendary bridge.

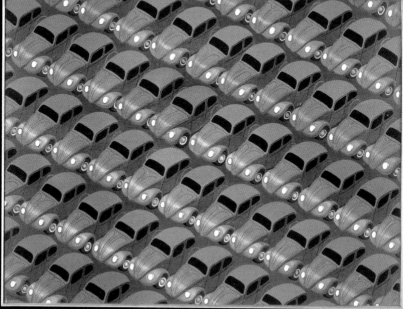

VW, IBM, BOEING &
LEWANDOWSKI-LOIS

MACHINE PAINTINGS 1957-1987   RICHARD GREEN GALLERY 152 WOOSTER ST.

LEWANDOWSKI-LOIS PAINTS MACHINES

This poster brands a 1987 retrospective of 30 years of my wife's paintings, whose main oeuvre is interpreting the mystique and power of industrial products and machinery. When Rosemary is asked "why machines?," she explains that her father, Joe Lewandowski, met Laura Godlewski in the late 1920s when they worked at a spark plug factory in Syracuse, New York (and sparks flew). See lewandowski-lois.com to view the elegant, powerful canvases she creates in between her role as a mom, yia-yia, and my beloved partner for 64 years. (The eye-popping VW's parading down the Champs-Elysées dramatized her displeasure with my helping sell "a Nazi car in a Jewish town" when I was an art director at Doyle Dane Bernbach.)

GEORGE LOIS
37 WEST 12TH STREET
NEW YORK NY 10011

TEL (212) 255-3213
FAX (646) 230-0183

GEORGE LOIS 37 WEST 12TH STREET NEW YORK NY 10011
TEL (212) 255-3213 FAX (212) 255-6601

NO, *LOIS* IS NOT A SHORTENED GREEK NAME!

My personal stationery and business card, using the variation of Didot Bodoni
that I designed and rendered for CBS Television in 1953.

AGIA SOPHIA

A HOLY PLACE VIOLATED

My Agia Sophia logo, designed in the same style as my Free Sophie slogan
(with the hand of Christ in the "O," from one of the mosaics
in the iconic cathedral) is a protest to the Turkish government to resurrect
Agia Sophia, the birthplace of the Christian Orthodox
faith, into a functioning place of worship under Greek Orthodox leadership
and control. Turkish authorities had desecrated and transformed
the holy place of worship into a Moslem mosque, and then into a museum.
My call to "Free Sophie" resonates with non-believers
(who believe in freedom of worship) as well as the faithful.

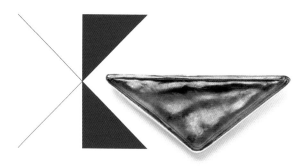

A LOGO FOR KIMBERLIN BROWN,
A JEWELER WITH AN EDGE

Kim Brown's passions give rebirth to the gorgeous stones she sources
from around the world, including diamonds, sapphires,
rubies, opals, and pearls, as well as the leftover Louis Comfort Tiffany
glass "jewels" produced for his lamps and interiors.
No wonder jewelery fashionistas all over the world liken
Kimberlin Brown to Botticelli's *The Birth of Venus*.
The geometric K and B design has become her jewelers mark.

FREE SOPHIE!

CHRISTIANDOM'S MOTHER CHURCH IS HELD CAPTIVE IN A TURKISH STRANGLEHOLD OF BIGOTRY AND DISCRIMINATION. 250 MILLION ORTHODOX CHRISTIANS AROUND THE WORLD DEMAND AGIA SOPHIA, THE SACRED EPICENTER OF THEIR RELIGION, BE SET FREE!

CHRIST, 12TH CENT., AGIA SOPHIA, 537 A.D. AFTER THE TURKISH CONQUEST OF CONSTANTINOPLE IN 1453, ALL CHRISTIAN MOSAICS WERE PLASTERED OVER AND THE RADIANT BIRTHPLACE OF THE CHRISTIAN ORTHODOX FAITH WAS DESECRATED AND TRANSFORMED INTO A MUSLIM MOSQUE. IN 1933 THE PLASTER WAS REMOVED AND THE DEPICTION OF CHRIST WAS RESURRECTED.

"**WOW** *I LOOK GOOD*"

WITH PATENTED, REVOLUTIONARY 3·D FIT TECHNOLOGY!

FIT TECHNOLOGY TO MAKE YOU LOOK LEANER

In showing a top American designer brand name samples of how 3·D fit technology gives women an undeniably leaner look, one of their female designers tried on a 3·D Fit top and 3·D Fit jeans, looked into a full-length mirror and cooed, *Wow, I look good!*

ADAM | LEVINE

FOR THE ADAM AND EVE'S OF THE WORLD
(Put something on, for God's sake!)

"LET US MAKE MAN IN OUR IMAGE"

An apparel line for both sexes by the sexy song writer, musician, entrepreneur and front man of Maroon 5. (But he didn't have the balls to use my logo.)

BRANDING THE PROTEST TO SAVE SAINT VINCENT'S HOSPITAL

Saint Vincent de Paul was a priest in the Catholic Church who spent his life serving the poor. Dedicated to the "Great Apostle of Charity," Saint Vincent's Hospital, in the Manhattan neighborhood of Greenwich Village, served millions of New Yorkers since 1849. In 2010, Saint Vincent's, a major teaching hospital with one of the busiest emergency rooms in town, was the target of a controversial billion-dollar luxury condo conversion plan by the Rudin real estate dynasty. After an anguished protest by neighborhood groups against the takeover, St. Vinnie is gone forever. Another sad example of business greed that benefits the wealthy at the expense of the poor and powerless.

St. Vincent is turning over in his Grave

We must stop
The Rudin Organization
from closing
Saint Vincent's Hospital
and leaving the
people of Greenwich Village
without healthcare!

MUSEUM OF PHOTOGRAPHY

THE MUSEUM OF PHOTOGRAPHY

A proposed museum of photography in New York City.
There are more than a dozen other museums throughout the world with a similar name.
So, being forced to live with the generic nature of the name,
my logo emphasizes THE, making it the visual focal point of a powerful, ever-changing logo.

MUSEUM OF PHOTOGRAPHY

Nicki Minaj

A STAR WITH CURVES

Nicki Minaj, the Trinidad-born American rapper, singer, songwriter, actress, and television personality, said she loved this logo, but she kissed it off.

A CATCHY LOGO

Jeremy Marshall, owner and head chef of Aquagrill, took his recipe of a traditional Lobster Roll, and mixing-in succulent shrimp, magically made it tastier and tenderer— so we named it— LobShrimp Roll.

LOBSHRIMP ROLL™
BY AQUAGRILL

"We're a helluva shellfish sandwich"

SHOP YOUR WAY BRANDS™

A MEANINGLESS NAME TRANSFORMED INTO ONE WITH CONCEPTUAL POWER

A lame name for a company that brands apparel for well-known celebrities, but I was stuck with it. But the finger pointing to the viewer suddenly made Shop Your Way Brands meaningful and personal.

FOR YOU!
AUTHENTIC PERSONAL STYLES OF ICONIC ARTISTS FROM THE MUSIC & ENTERTAINMENT WORLD

A BIG APPLE CHUTZPAH LOGO FOR MAYOR ED KOCH

A logo for a Gala Fundraising Roast asked (begged) the fat cats to pay the Mayor's enormous campaign debts in the 1981 Mayoralty election. In one bold stroke, I had hizzoner fess up and charm the power elite. The image became the talk of the town and packed the vast banquet room in Sheraton Centre. New York's shakers and movers emptied their pants pockets and strutted around all evening imitating the mayor. The money was raised and the slate was wiped clean.

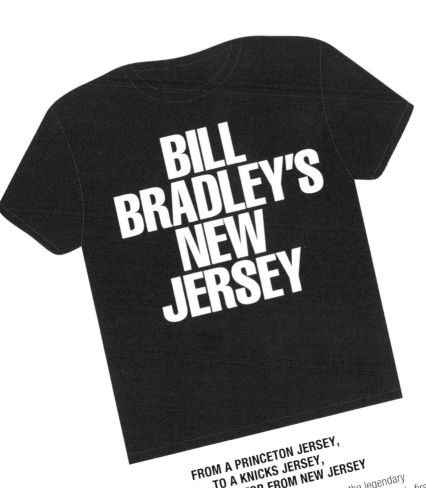

BILL BRADLEY'S NEW JERSEY

FROM A PRINCETON JERSEY,
TO A KNICKS JERSEY,
TO THE SENATOR FROM NEW JERSEY

My proposed logo and ad campaign in 1978 for the legendary Princeton All-American and New York Knicks basketball star, making his first run to become the U.S. Senator from the state of New Jersey. Inexplicably, the brilliant Rhodes scholar rejected my branding, but happily went on to win the campaign, going on to serve 18 productive years as a progressive United States senator. Years later, when I reminded him of his turning his back on my branding idea, Dollar Bill said, "Wow, why didn't I run with that?"

BRANDING MY
SEVEN YEAR ITCH

I left Papert Koenig Lois (the first ad agency I started in 1960) after seven years, and this put-on of Marilyn Monroe's legendary scene in *The Seven Year Itch* announced that I had spent another full seven years at my second agency, Lois Holland Callaway. The thrill seekers mobbed the TGI Gallery in Manhattan to see an exhibition of seven years of my legwork at LHC.

THE SEVEN YEAR ITCH
(7 HAPPY YEARS OF BLOOD SWEAT AND TEARS
BY LOIS HOLLAND CALLAWAY INC.)

ADDING POP TO
A SYMPHONY ORCHESTRA
(AND CLASS TO A POP SINGER)

In 1985, Timothy Galfas was asked to take a portrait of Pia Zadora for an album cover of her singing with The London Philharmonic Orchestra. He sent me a photo of her conducting in a tux, and I branded the album *Pia & Phil*. The alliteration of *Pia & Phil* received a ton of media attention, helping to make it one of the biggest selling albums of a great symphony orchestra. (And Pia Zadora earned the respect of music critics who had previously written her off.)

ELVIS
LIVES

BRANDING AN ETERNAL ICON

In my book, *Iconic America*, I nailed down the
eternal branding of the Elvis Presley
phenomenon with color-coding that graphically
makes clear that the word ELVIS,
and the word LIVES, are mystically related.

HOW TO TRANSFORM AN EXISTING, OLD-FASHIONED LOGO, AND MAKE IT EYE-SHATTERING AT POINT OF SALE

Christmas wraps in the booze business are the absolute worst, most pretentious, packages of all time. Holiday shelves become a field of fatuous pomp and circumstance, all phony glitz and all alike, all confirming the limitations of holly, wreaths, Santa, foil, ribbons, and the colors green and red. In 1973, my way to get drinkers to notice Cutty Sark in liquor stores during the holidays was to blow-up its funky label logo and wrap it around the box—instantly giving it a startling, avant-garde Pop Art look. Four boxes placed together on a shelf (or store window) created a blazing *poster* of a now somehow hip scotch. Cutty holiday sales almost doubled from any previous year. I'll drink to that.

READ ALL ABOUT IT: FOUNDED IN 1801 BY ALEXANDER HAMILTON!

When Peter Kalikow purchased the *New York Post* in 1988, I instantly changed the
Rupert Murdoch-inherited schlock image with the ad slogan, *A reassuring word to Alexander Hamilton,
the founder of the Post. Don't worry, your newspaper is in good hands!*
(It was news to New Yorkers that the *Post* had been founded in 1801 by Hamilton!) The new owner
let me redesign their masthead and type style throughout, keeping a tough
tabloid style but giving it some New York attitude and zip. When Mr. Murdoch repurchased the *Post*
in 1993, he allowed his Australian editor to kill our founding father,
Alexander Hamilton. (Dumb move, mate.)

**AFTER A DEAD RACOON WAS THROWN ON ANNA WINTOUR'S
PLATE AS SHE DINED AT THE FOUR SEASONS,
A MORE CIVIL ATTACK ON HER FEATURING
FUR IN VOGUE MAGAZINE**

In 1996, my campaign for Friends of Animals,
an animal advocacy organization
working to prevent cruelty
to animals throughout
the world.

ZIPbox™

**IF ANYONE TELLS YOU NOT TO BUY CEREAL
PACKAGED IN A ZIPBOX, TELL THEM TO ZIP IT!**

Introducing the freshest packaging idea in 50 years.
The ZIPbox press-to-close zipper provides an
airtight seal with easy open and close (eliminating the
need for a liner). After pouring your favorite
cereal into a bowl, no more crumpling up the liner
and shoving the bag down, then fumbling
with the thin paperboard flap that is not airtight.

REAL COWBOY
AND NATIVE AMERICAN
WEAR

ROY ROGERS
WESTERN
WEAR

ICONIC COWBOY...AND CHOCTAW!

In 2013, in resurrecting and rebranding America's beloved singing cowboy,
I enlisted Paul Davis, the legendary poster designer of Joseph Papp's Public Theater productions,
to portray Roy Rogers as both a cowboy and almost shockingly, as a Choctaw.
Although Rogers was immensely proud of his Choctaw ancestry, it was not publicized during those days
of the Jim Crow South with its rabid racism against African-Americans AND Native-Americans!

When I asked Paul to render the image, I had no idea he was the son of a Methodist Minister,
actually living in the Choctaw Nation of Oklahoma, and had grown up watching
Roy Rogers at the famous Pioneer Theater on many Saturday afternoons. Helping resurrect Rogers,
who was a champion for orphans and children of all races, including the fostering
of interracial adoption, was an act of love and respect for Paul Davis.

You don't have a cold!
I dode hab a code?
You have an allergy!
I hab an allergee?

It can sneeze like a cold, tear like a cold, sniff like a cold, cough like a cold, blow like a cold, feel like a cold—and still be an allergy. One way to tell: if you have 3 or more colds a year, the chances are good your cold is an allergy.* Take Allerest.

This new tablet calms the cough, the sneeze, the tears, the runny nose, the itchy eye of allergic colds. No cold tablet can work as well.

ALLEREST FOR ALLERGY

If you wake up sneezing, take Allerest. If you have 3 or more colds a year, take Allerest. If you... ah-ah-ah-choo? Take Allerest.

(*When you have a cold, you usually develop resistance that should protect you for some time. So if you have repeated colds, 3 or more a year, take Allerest. Your druggist has Allerest and will tell you about it.) 24 tablets for $1.25 · PHARMACRAFT LABORATORIES

ALLEREST FOR ALLERGY.
IN 1960, THE FIRST BRANDING FOR A
NON-PRESCRIPTION PRODUCT
TO ALLEVIATE THE SYMPTOMS OF ALLERGIES

It could sneeze like a cold, tear like a cold, sniff like a cold, cough like a cold, blow like a cold, feel like a cold – and still be an allergy.
The way to tell: if you have three or more colds a year – the cold is probably an allergy. (Because when you have a cold, you usually develop resistance that protects you for a good amount of time.)
One of many ads in the campaign, this is an example of visual Onomatopoeia (the use of words related to their sound).

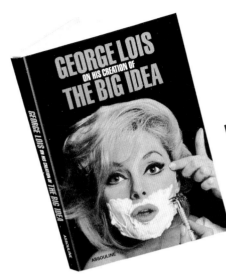

BIG IDEAS ARE NOT HEAVEN-SENT

Getting the Bid Idea is rooted
in the study of the collective conscious
of 7,000 years of human experience.
Known in the design world as "Mr. Big Idea,"
I traced over 100 of them back to
the genesis of each concept.

VOUCHERS?

CITIZENS COMMITTEE FOR PUBLIC INFORMATION ON VOUCHERS

THERE'S AN OUCH IN EVERY VOUCHER

A logo and ad campaign fighting the Voucher School Program
throughout America that hurts schools and students alike.

BRANDING PHONE MISER WITH THE IMAGE OF SCROOGE

In 1999, an ingenious device to protect consumers from
being ripped off on long-distance phone calls,
was a product we named PhoneMiser: Plugged into your
PC (keeping your current long-distance carrier),
PhoneMiser guaranteed the lowest cost on every call
made, with savings that slashed phone bills
up to 60%. The miserly Ebeneezer Scrooge taught us
all how to save a buck or two as a memorable
spokesman on TV and radio, in print,
and in-your-face packaging.

"Scrooge the Phone Company!"

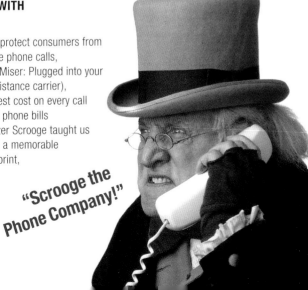

JUST BETWEEN US

TWEENS OF AMERICA, UNITE!

An interactive social venue website for the untapped market of 22 million tweens in America. Tweens all look forward to becoming teenagers, but for those awkward years before they do, just between us, they can feel like they are part of something new, original and strong.

HOW TO STOP A COMPETITIVE BRAND DEAD IN ITS TRACKS

In 1984, when the Turner Broadcasting System announced a middle-of-the-road knockoff of MTV, their shocked honchos and I said, "Ted, stop the music!" And VH-1 was born in a day! Bob Pittman, the driving force of MTV, called me with the news: Ted Turner was ripping-off the MTV business model, and with a popular music category that could attract millions of traditional music fans in America. What to do? How do we head Turner off at the pass? Turner could not be allowed to steal our thunder! In an hour of rapid-fire decision-making, we would announce, within a few days, in music and advertising trade papers, that VH-1 was well on its way, brand name and logo, infrastructure, sales team, marketing plan, and ad campaign intact. When the first ad ran, Turner's network was dead in the water – one of the most outrageous accomplishments in competitive marketing history – and VH-1 became one of Viacom's biggest moneymakers.

VH-1

VIDEO HITS ONE

"Boy, what a bunch of Newsbreakers!"

WITH BALL-BREAKING BRANDING, A NEWS SHOW GOES FROM WORST TO FIRST

In 1979, Channel 2 News was dead last in news ratings in the metropolitan area. I changed their utilitarian nomenclature from Channel 2 News... to *The Channel 2 Newsbreakers*, with the clear implication in wise-ass TV spots that "Newsbreakers" was a cleaned up version of "ball-breakers." (It helped that their lead anchor, Jim Jensen, was known to be a hard-ass throughout the news industry.) My ad campaign called their broadcast area *Newsbreaker Territory*, and their 22 male and female on-air team took their new moniker to heart, becoming "the biggest bunch of Newsbreakers anywhere," an aggressive, street-smart, street-tough, newsbreaking crew. *The Channel 2 Newsbreakers* leapfrogged to No. 1 in no time and remained the leading news show in the metropolitan area for the five years they kept my brand name.

The Channel ⊙2 Newsbreakers

BRANDING ROBERT MOSES A SINNER

In 1962, New York's Highway Commissioner Robert Moses, the master broker who constructed highways in, out, over, under, and through New York with little concern for mass transit needs, decreed that a four-lane highway was needed to carry cars across the 20-mile length of Fire Island. Plans were drawn to construct the highway right through the skinny line of summer homes on Fire Island. It would turn an idyllic community into a California Freeway. Moses' scheme seemed like a fait accompli. My family had recently discovered this perfect summer place to raise two young boys, and my wife Rosie got mad as hell and organized the Tenants Committee to Save Fire Island to prevent the Moses road. (The homeowners were organized. Ain't they always?) To help her win the battle, I did this poster. It was my eleventh commandment for Moses. I wanted our neighbors and the powers that be to understand that God had more authority than Moses. I produced dozens of large posters as picket signs for Rosie and her committee. And boy, did they picket. Armed with the might of the hand of an accusing god, Rosie's housewives told Moses at a public hearing where to get off! The road was never built.

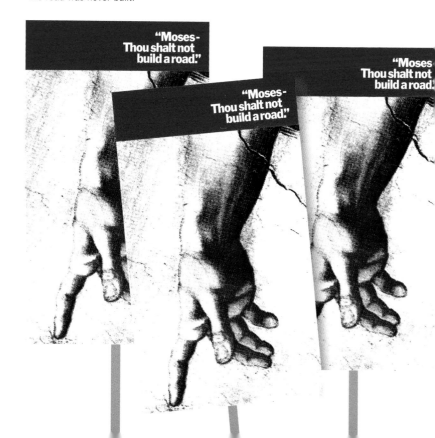

DATRIL PM

NON-ASPIRIN PAIN RELIEVER
PROMOTES RESTFUL SLEEP

THE GENESIS OF THE FIRST "PM" BRAND EXTENSION IN MARKETING HISTORY

In 1969, knowing of my reputation a resurrector of failing brands, the top honcho
at Bristol-Myers asked me to come up with an idea to energize
their Datril brand, which had become a financial headache. "Can you combine
a headache and a sleeping pill and call it Datril PM," I asked.
He seemed stunned, and said he would talk to his R&D people. One night, six months
later, I saw a Bristol-Myers TV commercial, produced by their
largest ad agency, introducing Excedrin PM, a line extension of their successful
Excedrin brand. Excedrin business catapulted and "night time"
PM products became a worldwide marketing approach. No good deed goes unpunished.

"Moses -
Thou shalt not
build a road."

TIMELESS WHOPPERS THAT WILL LIVE FOREVER

The Nation's founding prospectus of 1865 focuses on "waging war upon the vices of violence, exaggeration and misrepresentation." The founders refrained from biting the bullet – they're called *lies*. Calling out misinformation and lies to the American people, as always, remains the focus of *The Nation's* mission. So beginning in August 2012, with 40 full-page weekly editorials, I immortalized what I called *Timeless Whoppers* – and that's no lie.

HOW TO MAKE
PICKLED GREEN BEANS FAMOUS

In 1960, two smart young women were stinking up the neighborhood by pickling raw string beans in 400-lb. barrels of vinegar and dill. Named Dilly Beans, they hoped their product would be a gourmet item. With a tiny budget of $30,000 and ads like this beauty holding a Dilly Bean like a cigarette as though she was going to take a puff, they became famous, and within a few years sold their business for a cool $2 million bucks. *Time* magazine wrote a lengthy article and said, "The Dilly Beans success is a tribute to the power of advertising."

A GREAT SLOGAN BRINGS A BRAND NAME TO LIFE

Stuck all alone on the marina side of Atlantic City, far from where a phalanx of nine casinos were packing them in, Harrah's top-of-mind awareness among Atlantic City goers was 1%, with gaming revenues dead last. To build immediate brand recognition while communicating the soul and spirit of Harrah's, I adopted the famous musical theme *I'm just wild about Harrah's* (based on the classic, *I'm just wild about Harry*) with Susan Anton belting it out in TV spots. Within three weeks, Harrah's became the best-known casino in Atlantic City, with gaming revenues zooming to second place.

WORN BY CUSTOMERS...

WORN BY EMPLOYEES

BRANDING THE FLAVOR OF MILAN
IN THE PAN AM BUILDING

For a spiffy Italian restaurant, Tony Palladino, my old high school chum, and I, created a powerful logotype that synthesized the great Milanese design tradition. For the restaurant's interior, we created striking screens that were montages of dozens of logotypes of bellissimo Italian food products (Bartolini, Bertolli, Lochitello, Pasta di Stiglino, Prunotto, etc.) that stylistically complimented our bold Trattoria logo, all the while enthusiastically approved under the watchful eye of the iconic Bauhaus architect of the Pan Am building, Walter Gropius.

The Shampoo that Kenneth uses. (for dry hair)

NET. WT. 7 OZ.

LEAN CUISINE

STOUFFER'S DEVOURED MY NAME (BUT CANNED MY LOGO)

This is my original logo design for Lean Cuisine, a conceptually perfect visualization of the meaning of the two-word, euphonious brand name I created for Stouffer's in 1977. They had rejected producing a revolutionary, frozen gourmet fitness food line, but were ecstatic about the marketing possibility when they saw the name Lean Cuisine. But inexplicably, they replaced my design with a non-descript, uncommunicative, traditional typeface. But even without my pluperfect logo, it was one of the great marketing successes of the decade.

"GEORGE, DESIGN A PACKAGE THAT SAYS 'KENNETH'"

Kenneth was the most famous hair stylist in the world. He styled Marilyn Monroe's hair before she sang "Happy Birthday, Mr. President"... and he cut Jackie Kennedy's hair at 7:00 am before she left with her husband for Dallas on that fateful day of November 21, 1963. In 1968, everybody we talked to at Kenneth's seven-story beauty salon in New York called his superb shampoo, "the shampoo that Kenneth uses." So, I designed a package with that five-word, memorable name.

THE SIX BEST MAYORS IN AMERICA:
Alioto of San Francisco
who increases services but lowers taxes.

I'm voting for one of the 6 best mayors in America.

Massell of Atlanta
the fastest growing city
in the South.

Landrieu of New Orleans
who preserved
the splendid French Quarter.

White of Boston
who brought city government
back to his people.

Maier of Milwaukee
whose sensible curfew defused
a riot situation.

And our own Lee Alexander
for making Syracuse New York's only
major city that isn't broke. We consider him
one of the six best Mayors in America.
Let's make him our Mayor again.

I BRANDED LEE ALEXANDER OF SYRACUSE "ONE OF THE SIX BEST MAYORS IN AMERICA" (AND MY OUTRAGEOUS POLITICAL CLAIM BECAME A SELF-FULFILLING PROPHECY)

In 1973, Lee Alexander was running for a second term as mayor of Syracuse. He was an activist liberal in a decidedly conservative town and the polls showed he was going to get clobbered. So I did a campaign that ordained five other American mayors, and, of course... Lee Alexander of Syracuse, as *The Six Best Mayors in America!* Whether or not he was or wasn't one of the six best mayors in America became the issue of the campaign, and his confused, blind-sided opponent spent most of his time tripping over himself, arguing that Alexander wasn't. In no time, his campaign to insist that Syracuse *wasn't* one of the six best-governed cities in America, became an affront to civic pride! Finally the leading Republican newspapers in Syracuse both admitted editorially that perhaps Syracuse's own Lee Alexander *was* one of the six best mayors in America! In a conservative Republican town, Alexander was reelected by a whopping 68% of Syracuse voters.

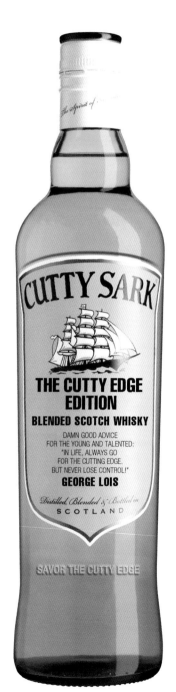

SAVOR THE CUTTY EDGE

In 2014, inspired by a new generation at Cutty Sark that discovered my outrageous 1973 *Don't give up the ship* ad campaign, I was asked to brand a special edition of their blended Scotch whisky. As a progenitor of cutting edge design and communications, I branded it, on their classic yellow label, The Cutty Edge Edition.
Hold fast.
Sip steady.
Savor the Cutty Edge.

SCOTT OF PA.

THE MOST
POWERFUL SENATOR
PENNSYLVANIA
EVER HAD.

MY ANTI-NIXON CAMPAIGN

When I asked Senate Minority Leader Hugh Scott how I could possibly explain to my descendants
that during the Nixon Administration I helped to reelect the top Republican to the
Senate, he answered, "Tell them this. The only thing that separated Richard Nixon from Fascism…
was Hugh Scott." I went to work for him with relish, calling him *Scott of Pennsylvania*,
a heroic image in the genre of Lincoln of Illinois and Charles de Gaulle. He needed a decisive vote
of at least 100,000 to remain Minority Leader, because Nixon was gunning for him.
He won by 220,000 and the good senator went on to help torpedo Nixon.

HOW CUTE CAN YOU GET?

A stylized logo of
3 Little Kittens shows
how cuteness can
make pussycat owners purr.

The Chep Chepmunk

MY CHEEKY CHEPMUNK

To convince industry to convert to
environmentally friendly Chep USA
wooden pallets (rather than
plastic), an animated, Disney-like,
chip off the ol' block
Chepmunk logo and mascot.

THE EVER-CHANGING LOGOTYPE

In 1983, I created the Nickelodeon logo, which,
like a kid's imagination, could be a zillion
and one different versions. So Dennis Mazzella,
my long-time, right-hand man, designed
a bomb, a guitar, an egg, a turkey, a smile, etc.
From that day, the only way you can tell
a real Nick logo from an imposter is – the
shape is always orange!

A DOG'S BEST FRIEND:
K9H2O!

A name and logo for an all-natural drink,
loaded with vitamins to compensate
for any deficiencies in a dog's daily diet.
(The pup on the label is Karma,
once the faithful sidekick of my son
Luke and his family.)

YOU NEVER SAUSAGE A LOGO!

(For gemultnicht snack bars where Bavarian sausages were made
and smoked daily, served by plump blonde fräuleins.)

A BEE-YOUTIFUL LOGO

for a PR company.
The Queen Bee is a Mycenaean
gold pendant (1,500 BC),
a 50th anniversary present
to my honey.

Buzz Creative Group

PUSS'N BOOTS COMES TO LIFE

with a knapsack over his
shoulder filled with Puss'n Boots cat
food, stepping out for a stroll.

BRANDING ALEXANDER'S BY SHOWING SAVVY NEW YORK WOMEN SINGING AT THE FRONT ENTRANCE OF THEIR POSH COMPETITORS

In 1982, Alexander's department store had been a fixture of New York's frenetic retail scene. Research showed that their image was lousy, but female shoppers loved their special values – and that many women bought their cloths at Alexander's, but replaced the labels with ones from a fancy-schmancy store. So I filmed commercials of classy women shoppers singing their hearts at the actual front entrances of Bloomingdale's, Tiffany's, Saks, Macy's, Bergdorf,etc. The ad campaign transformed Alexander's image overnight, and the owners sang our praises.

WOMAN SINGS:

I browse at Bloomingdale's
I breakfast at Tiffany's
But I buy at Alexander's!
I buy at Alexander's!

I'm sauntering through Saks
Meandering through Macy's
But I buy at Alexander's!
I buy at Alexander's!

I never forget to go to the Met
But I buy at Alexander's!
I buy at Alexander's!

SHAKING UP AMERICA

A revolutionary, instant heating technology in totally portable containers of coffees, teas and soups, are shaking up America.

AN IROQUOIS MASTERPIECE

For Bear Mountain Inn, this 19th century Iroquois image of an expressive bear adds an historical reference to a rustic weekend spot just 45 miles north of the Big Apple.

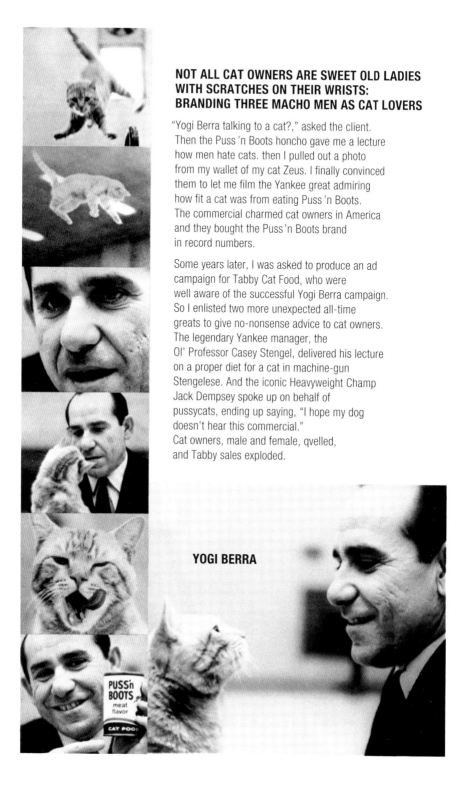

NOT ALL CAT OWNERS ARE SWEET OLD LADIES WITH SCRATCHES ON THEIR WRISTS: BRANDING THREE MACHO MEN AS CAT LOVERS

"Yogi Berra talking to a cat?," asked the client. Then the Puss 'n Boots honcho gave me a lecture how men hate cats. then I pulled out a photo from my wallet of my cat Zeus. I finally convinced them to let me film the Yankee great admiring how fit a cat was from eating Puss 'n Boots. The commercial charmed cat owners in America and they bought the Puss 'n Boots brand in record numbers.

Some years later, I was asked to produce an ad campaign for Tabby Cat Food, who were well aware of the successful Yogi Berra campaign. So I enlisted two more unexpected all-time greats to give no-nonsense advice to cat owners. The legendary Yankee manager, the Ol' Professor Casey Stengel, delivered his lecture on a proper diet for a cat in machine-gun Stengelese. And the iconic Heavyweight Champ Jack Dempsey spoke up on behalf of pussycats, ending up saying, "I hope my dog doesn't hear this commercial." Cat owners, male and female, qvelled, and Tabby sales exploded.

YOGI BERRA

PUSS'n BOOTS meat flavor

CAT FOOD

THE WRITE STUFF

A website offering a penorama of pen styles for personalized giveaways
for the business world in building their brand imagery.
Hey, you can always use an extra pen or two.

PEN-O-RAMA.COM

CASEY STENGEL

JACK DEMPSEY

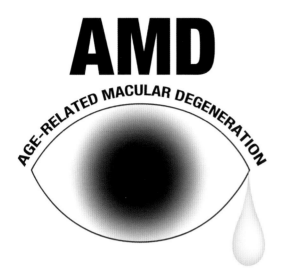

A LOGO REALISTICALLY DEPICTING AMD

Age-related Macular Degeneration (AMD) is a leading cause of vision loss in Americans' 60 years of age and older, and a leading cause of irreversible blindness and visual impairment in the world. The number of people living with AMD today is as great as the number of those who have all types of invasive cancer.

"YOU ARE LEGALLY BLIND"

With these four words Jim Hindman, renowned entrepreneur and founder of Jiffy Lube International, would face the biggest challenge of his life at age 57 when he was diagnosed with Age-related Macular Degeneration. The unvanquished Jim Hindman became a staunch pioneer in bringing attention to new medical procedures and technologies that miraculously restored his vision with Implantable Miniature Telescope surgery. This book I named and designed, tells his remarkable story. Was blind, but now he sees.

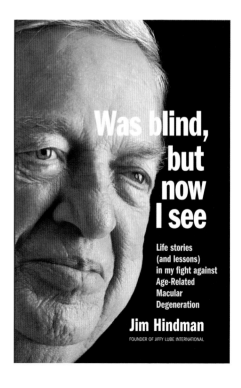

Was blind, but now I see

Life stories (and lessons) in my fight against Age-Related Macular Degeneration

Jim Hindman
FOUNDER OF JIFFY LUBE INTERNATIONAL

Time to $ave

WHEN TIMES GET TOUGH, ITS TIME TO SAVE

Richard Minervino, a multi-successful entrepreneur all his life, was intent on creating a revolution of financial education across the globe. So he created Time to $ave, a loyalty shopping plan with the benefits of discounts, rebates, a percentage of the purchase price directly deposited into your own personal retirement account, and to top it all off, an automatic donation to a charity of your choice! Now *that's* a Big Idea.

MORE IS MORE

Two new logos on one can of Tabby Cat Food:

An ampersand turned into a cat – ears and tail included – plus a Tabby logo with a sweeping pussycat tail!

(If you don't love cats, you won't love these logos.)

Counting today, I have sat in prison 3,135 days for a crime I did not commit.

If I don't get a re-trial, I have 289 years to go. Six months ago the 'eyewitnesses' who testified they saw me leaving a bar in which 3 people had been killed, admit they gave false testimony. Despite this, the judge who sentenced me won't give me a re-trial. Why?

**RUBIN HURRICANE CARTER
NO. 45472
TRENTON STATE PRISON**

THE OPENING SALVO IN ENLISTING CELEBRITIES TO WAGE A GUERILLA WAR ACCUSING JERSEY AUTHORITIES FOR RAILROADING AN INNOCENT MAN

In 1975, I showed this tiny ad to Rubin "Hurricane" Carter the first day I visited him in the slammer. I ran it in the news section of the national edition of *The New York Times* a few days later. The whole country was buzzing about this unprecedented (and outrageous) ad from a convicted killer in prison, appealing for help. In two weeks time, Muhammad Ali and I enlisted 75 celebrities, all moved by Rubin Carter's plea.

BEHIND BARS, RUBIN CARTER, STUNNINGLY, SPEAKS TO THE SPORTS WORLD

This image of Hurricane Carter is from a film I produced of him in his tiny cell in Trenton State Prison, and shown to over 200 reporters the morning of the Muhammad Ali – Ron Lyle heavyweight championship bout. I had filmed it surreptitiously, under the very nose of the prison authorities. Media all over America was totally stunned by the appearance of the man they knew was incarcerated with a 300 year jail term for supposedly murdering three white men in a bar in Patterson New Jersey in 1966.

The only innocent Hurricane!

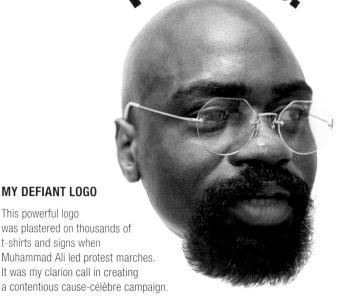

MY DEFIANT LOGO

This powerful logo
was plastered on thousands of
t-shirts and signs when
Muhammad Ali led protest marches.
It was my clarion call in creating
a contentious cause-célèbre campaign.

BOB DYLAN JOINS THE PROTEST

Bob Dylan wrote the explosive protest song,
Hurricane, and we produced a *Night of the Hurricane*
concert in Madison Square Garden, as
20,000 screaming fans, along with Muhammad Ali
and our intrepid committee,
proudly wore this button.

THE RUBIN CARTER CASE BECAME FAMOUS WORLDWIDE, AND IN 1985 HE WAS A FREE MAN

Finally, a federal District court
threw out his conviction and in 1988,
a U.S. District court, citing
"grave constitutional violations,"
upheld the noble ruling that
Rubin Carter had been unjustly
convicted in a vicious act of
racism. Truly, Rubin Carter was proven
the only "Innocent Hurricane."

BRANDING THE NEW PROPRIETORS OF THE FOUR SEASONS "THE TWO-OF-US," REGAINS ITS STATURE BY CREATING TWO SUPERSTAR OWNERS

The '70s were shaping up as the disaster decade for New York's great restaurants. And by 1974, the 15-year-old Four Seasons restaurant was losing money and sliding toward extinction. It was perceived, increasingly, as a "tourist" restaurant, forsaking its power-base Manhattan clientele, and was regarded by the restaurant industry as a white elephant. With all these odds stacked against them, Tom Margittai and Paul Kovi bravely bought The Four Seasons and asked me to somehow change the perception of the once magnificent restaurant in the minds and hearts of the shakers and movers of the Big Apple. So I boldly positioned the new owners as "The-two-of-us" shaking hands in front of their "store," and ran a full-page ad in *The New York Times*. The ad charmed New York food lovers who valued the magnificent interior, great cuisine, service, ambiance and most importantly, the promise that Margittai and Kovi were there day and night, running the show. Overnight, New Yorkers flocked back and the two Hungarian expatriates became the hottest restaurateurs in America.

SETTING THE TABLE FOR DIPLOMACY

The Chief of Protocol at The State Department asked for a logo to dramatize Secretary of State Hillary Clinton's vision of involved diplomacy by utilizing food, hospitality and the dining experience as a diplomatic tool that could engage foreign dignitaries, bridge cultures and strengthen relationships.
They didn't bite.

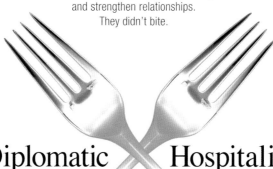

Diplomatic ╳ Hospitality

COMMON GOALS
STRENGTHENING RELATIONSHIPS
BRIDGING CULTURES

"The two-of-us"

TOM MARGITTAI

PAUL KOVI

Dear Dick Tiger:

Here's why I think
I deserve
a crack at your
middleweight crown:
The last time we fought,
I beat you!

Respectfully,
Joey Archer

Dear Dick Tiger:

The Middleweight
Champion should meet
the best middleweight
(not a welterweight).
I'm a middleweight,
and I licked every man
I ever fought, including you.

Respectfully,
Joey Archer

P.S.
(How about a fight, Dick?
I'm going broke
on these ads.)

BRANDING DICK TIGER *CHICKEN* FOR REFUSING TO FIGHT MY PAL FROM THE BRONX

In 1966, Bronxite Joey Archer was trying to get a shot at the middleweight crown. The champ, Nigerian Dick Tiger, wanted nothing to do with Archer, a good boxer with a reputation as a spoiler. Tiger was planning a rematch with Emile Griffith, a welterweight. So I ran two small ads – they were miniscule, but they knocked the fight fans out. The first $200 ad started the commotion (*The Daily News* put Joey on their front page, challenging a snarling tiger through the bars at the Bronx Zoo), and the second ad churned it into a furor. Finally, the brouhaha forced an elimination bout! A Griffith–Archer rematch was set at Madison Square Garden, the fight was a sellout, and I bet a bundle on Joey Archer. He lost.

DESIGNING A LOGO (AND SPREADING THE WORD)

In 1957, when Upjohn recognized that higher doses of ascorbic acid contributed greatly to the effectiveness of their therapeutic vitamin-mineral formula, I made the news memorable with a visually active logo.

UNICAP

DOUBLE
THE AMOUNT
OF THE
VITAMIN C

BREAK A LEG

A LOGO FOR A THEATER MAGAZINE

The actor, that puzzling blend of over-confidence and insecurity,
of superstition just this side of paranoia, has long believed
that a harmless salute of "good luck!" invited theatrical disaster.
To replace that innocent wish, thespians long ago came up with
"Break a Leg!" I choose that lighthearted curse unlikely to come true,
as a brand name for a prospective magazine on the liveliest of
the arts, the Theater: the gossip, the innuendo, and the delicious truth
about the denizens of showbiz, worldwide.

CHANGING THE NAME SLOMIN'S...TO THE SLOMIN'S SHIELD

Slomin's Security System needed a breakthrough ad campaign. Their shield logo was
screaming for a new, powerful name – The Slomin's Shield! They resisted me
for months, but they finally caved in. The authority of their fresh new name lent
credence to my TV spots of families singing, *Shield your home:
The Slomin's Shield!* Their business more than quadrupled, and the
owners of Slomin's made out like thieves.
To add some muscle to the shield logo,
Alarmo came to the rescue and
sales *really* went through the roof.

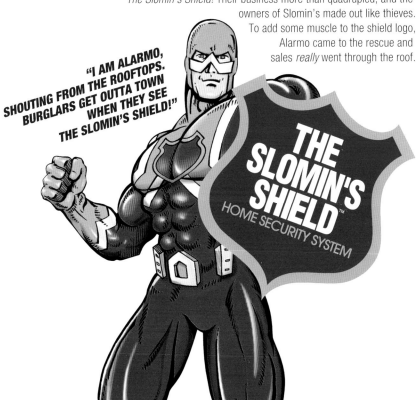

"I AM ALARMO,
SHOUTING FROM THE ROOFTOPS.
BURGLARS GET OUTTA TOWN
WHEN THEY SEE
THE SLOMIN'S SHIELD!"

THE SLOMIN'S SHIELD™
HOME SECURITY SYSTEM

WHAT A DIFFERENCE A NAME MAKES!

By moving a tiny slider on the bridge of revolutionary Superfocus glasses, you can focus on the page of a book, a computer screen, a movie, or a distant mountain – miraculously restoring the sight of your youth. Custom-made to your prescription, now you can see the world...in Superfocus! Originally named Trufocals, my new Superfocus brand name instantly helped make these brilliantly engineered glasses, certified by NASA for space flight for the use of astronauts on the Space Shuttle and International Space Station, and given the *Wall Street Journal* 2010 Technology Innovation Silver Award, an eye-popping marketing success.

Bauhaus

I branded this style of Superfocus glasses Bauhaus, in appreciation of the iconic movement created by design master Walter Gropius in Weimar in the 1920s. The Bauhaus has been a profound worldwide influence in art, architecture, graphic design, and last by not least, product design. I believe that Dr. Gropius would have approved of the sleek, utilitarian look of these Superfocus glasses.

FOCUS ™

E THE WORLD, FAR AND NEAR, IN SUPERFOCUS!

Corbu

I proudly branded these Superfocus glasses, Corbu, named after Le Corbusier, one of the great pioneers of modern architecture, as well as an urban planner, painter, sculptor, and modern furniture designer. His signature look was his famous, round, dark-rimmed glasses, with the temples centered on the circular rims. Look familiar?
(The big difference is that a Corbu wearer in the 21st century, will see the world...in Superfocus!)

Be a winner: loozit!

WHY BE A WEIGHT WATCHER WHEN YOU CAN JUST LOOZIT!

A no-nonsense weight management program that makes you lean and mean.

BRANDING A FRENCH PICNIC IN MANHATTAN

During lunch, dinner and after-theater at the Brasserie, residing in the great Seagram Building in Manhattan, a floor under The Four Seasons restaurant, you couldn't squeeze in one more beautiful person. So in the early 1960s, with the great restaurateur Joe Baum at the helm, we dreamed up an elegant French picnic take-out basket. The wicker basket was such a great success, I had to figure out a more economical way to have the picnic delivered and still exude the charm of a French picnic in Central Park, or in a board room of the General Motors building. This French flag-draped, fold-out box, loaded with the most delicious fast-food ever created, did the trick.

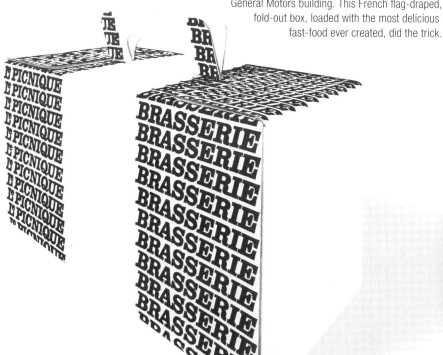

"I want my

MTV"

MUSIC TELEVISION

BRINGING A LOGO (AND A CULTURAL PHENOMENON) TO LIFE

After its first year of operations, MTV was an abject failure.
The MTV logo was initially created by Manhattan Design in 1981,
but a year later I brought it to life with the insertion
of the Rolling Stone logo, rock stars, rocket ships, etc.
Then I convinced Mick Jagger, in a TV spot,
to pick up a phone and bellow *I want my MTV* to the cable
operators of America. Thousands of young
rock fans mimicked Mick and the cable honchos
caved in. Almost immediately, MTV became the
most spectacular pop culture phenomenon in TV history.

STOLEN ART FROM STOLEN LIVES

THE MAUERBACH BENEFIT SALE
CHRISTIE'S
OCTOBER 29-30, 1996

**BRANDING AN AUCTION IN VIENNA OF ART,
STOLEN BY HITLER AND HIS SS OFFICIALS, TO BENEFIT
THE VICTIMS OF THE HOLOCAUST**

Like few victims in history, they lost all.
During the Nazi's brutal ethnic and cultural rampage, they were robbed of everything.
Identity. Dignity. Life. And yet the art they loved and lived with endures.
Some 8,000 objects of art remained after thousands of pieces were claimed by original
Jewish owners and family members. The Christie's auctioneer said
that throughout the sale, "the previous owners were never far from the minds
of the people in the room. There was a great recognition that we
were seeing again work that graced the walls of a culture Hitler had destroyed."

A MODERNIZED ALBRECHT DÜRER SIGNATURE MONOGRAM FOR THE ART DIRECTORS CLUB OF NEW YORK

I designed this 1958 Art Directors Club Annual from front cover
to back when I was the Consumer Art Director of Sudler & Hennessy
where the legendary Herb Lubalin was the head art director.
The spiffy rendering of my design was lettered by John Pistilli.

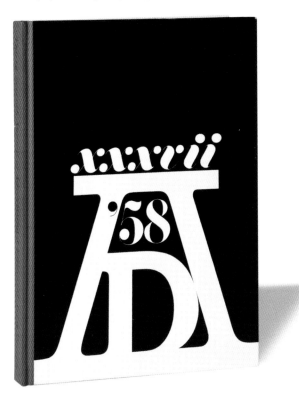

THE INSPIRATION FOR THE BRANDING OF THE ART DIRECTORS CLUB YEARLY AWARD SHOW

In the mid-1960s, in a discussion about our
approach to design, Massimo Vignelli summed up
the ethos of his life by saying, "George,
if you do it right, it will live forever." Half a century
later, in his last days in a hospice situation,
nobly sitting at his pristinely beautiful Vignelli table,
I reached out to Massimo, held his hands
and whispered, "Massimo, of course you were
right—but you were two words short.
You should have said:
'If you do it right, it, *and you*, will live forever.'"

Immortality for Your Work

ESPN WAS PERCEIVED AS A JUNK SPORTS NETWORK...UNTIL AMERICA'S GREATEST ATHLETES SHOVED ESPN IN YOUR FACE!

In 1990, I cajoled 15 of America's greatest sports stars to appear in ESPN commercials for zilch.
(For instance, Houston Oiler quarterback Warren Moon, with a bright moon behind him, leans in and says "When the moon comes out, ESPN is in your face.")
In a short time, ESPN was transformed into the power network of sports. The results of the branding campaign were, in the words of an ESPN executive, "a Harvard Business School case study on how to turn around a company's image."

THE LION KING OF WALL STREET

In 1958, DDB art director Bob Gage created the imagery of the Dreyfus Lion for The Dreyfus Fund. Thirty years later, from 1978 to 1986, in full page ads with bold, stark graphic power, challenging *The New York Times* restrictions on graphic design on their morbid financial pages (they were called "Tombstone ads"), their managed assets increased from $3 billion to $30 billion! A substantial share of those revenues were generated from my creation of a quarterly newsletter that I branded, *Letter from the Lion*, written and edited by my ad agency partner, Bill Pitts.

IN 1999, CYPRUS CRIES OUT
AGAINST 25 YEARS OF TURKISH OCCUPATION

An ad campaign and poster depicting a young Cypriot athlete,
sculpted in the 5th century BC (grandly residing
in the Cyprus Museum in Nicosia, in the unoccupied portion of Cyprus),
still weeps for Cyprus after more than
40 years of Turkish tyranny.

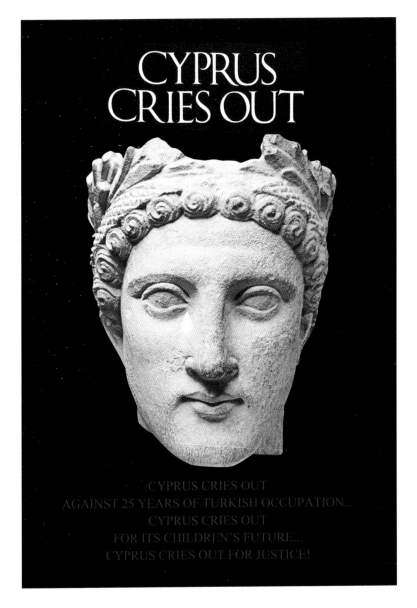

COLUMBUS PLANTED IT IN THE NEW WORLD,
NEIL ARMSTRONG AND BUZZ ALDRIN PLANTED IT ON THE MOON...

A logo dramatically seeking franchise buyers and realty salespeople (who have the right stuff) to fulfill their life's ambitions by joining an innovative commercial real estate brokerage firm to inspire small business owners to plant their flag in exciting, efficient workspace.

THE ULTIMATE LEARNING EXPERIENCE

Since 1900, when the Nobel Foundation was established, 19 billion human beings have lived, with only 835 Nobel Laureates among them. These men and women epitomize the ultimate achievements of the human mind. In 2008, Dr. Edward Shapiro, a Russian-American scientist, engineer and inventor has brought the Nobel Laureates to high schools to teach, inspire, and mentor young Americans.

Even the visionary
Alfred Noble
could not have
imagined his
Nobel Laureates
passionately
teaching in
the high schools
of America!

"Wow!"

NOBEL LAUREATES
SCHOOL VISITS

The Hooters

Anna Moffo

k Hawkins

Wolf Trap

sets you free

James McCracken

AMERICA'S FIRST NATIONAL PARK FOR THE PERFORMING ARTS

In 1977, a defining logo, slogan and graphic imagery for Wolf Trap, where the world's greatest popular and classical entertainers perform, indoors and out, for thousands of relaxed, picnicking people. Wolf Trap in beautiful Vienna, Virginia, 30 minutes from Washington DC. has been thrilling audiences for almost 50 years.

America's roast beef yes sir!

A LOGO
A SONG
AN AD CAMPAIGN
YES SIR!

A definitive design that spells out precisely what Arby's offers.

A SHARP LOGO FOR THE GENERIC SOUNDING "CONSUMERS EDGE"

I had to keep the Consumers Edge name, but my single-edge razor blade visual, along with a credit card in the shape of a razor blade titled, "The Edge" made it a memorable, cutting edge name.

CONSUMERS EDGE
INTERNATIONAL, LLC

CUT YOUR COSTS OF EVERYDAY PRODUCTS!

FIT FOR THE LIPS OF THE GODS ON MOUNT OLYMPUS

Every yogurt in America screams that they are Greek. But Loi is the authentic Greek yogurt, made by the Greek goddess of cuisine, Maria Loi (my cousin, a famous chef in Greece, who came to America in 2011 and opened Loi Restaurant in Manhattan). The ancient Greek coin depicts the goddess Artemis, the name of her mother, who taught her, step by step, how to make Greek yogurt fit for the lips of the gods on Mount Olympus! Maria's yogurt was famous in the area of Navpaktos, where the majority of the people in our villages live well into their 90s, with a cuisine based on olive oil for cooking and daily servings of yogurt.

GARBO SPOTTED IN MANHATTAN!

A proposal to a Swedish hotel company to celebrate the legendary career of the unforgettable Greta Garbo, the incomparable Swedish film actress and international star during Hollywood's silent and classic periods, by founding and naming a hotel named, The Garbo, in the actresses' adopted city. The Swedish screen icon became a naturalized citizen of the U.S. after she left Hollywood and spent the rest of her life in Manhattan (known for taking long, daily walks, sometimes dressed in slacks, and sporting large sunglasses, as "Garbo-watching" became a sport for all hip New Yorkers).

"SOME WOMEN SHOULD NEVER WEAR SLACKS!"

COPYWRITER RITA SELDEN, PAPERT KOENIG LOIS

FOR THE SLACKS DIVISION OF EVAN-PICONE:
THE MOST NEGATIVE BRANDING SLOGAN IN FASHION HISTORY

In 1963, Charles and Bob Evans of Evan-Picone were flourishing, but their slack sales were drooping. My new branding slogan came from the lips of Rita Selden (who had created the iconic VW "Lemon" ad when we both worked at Doyle Dane Bernbach). Babbling a mile a minute about womens' fashions of the day, she squeezed in her take on (some) women wearing slacks. Bingo! The audacity of her statement convinced women (who thought they had good figures) to go to Evan-Picone and insist on filling their wardrobe with slacks. Go figure.

Duck, Doc!

HERE COMES THE RAC ATTACK!

**TO PROTECT THE DEDICATED
DOCTORS OF AMERICA**

against the Recovery Audit Contractor's
"bounty hunter program," Fi-Med organized
a stirring, informative, blow-by-blow
2011 Physicians RAC Summit of leading
healthcare authorities in Orlando,
Florida, in January 2011. My theme and
logo, *Duck, Doc!* was a dire warning
to every physician in America.
(My cardiologist, Dr. William Cole,
volunteered to take one
for the team.)

Defending the Devil
and the American Way of Life

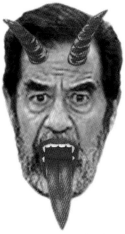

by Ramsey Clark

A PATRIOT IN DEFENSE OF A DEVIL

Ramsey Clark served as United States General under LBJ in 1967-1969. After leaving public office, Clark led many progressive activism campaigns, courageously offering legal defense to controversial figures, including the hated Saddam Hussein. As an admirer of his defense of the American institution of providing absolutely fair trials, even to the most heinous of criminals, I named his book, *Defending the Devil*, in which he eloquently explained why defending Hussein was in line with what he stood for all his life. Though he knew he would be viciously attacked, he knew it was the right thing to do. (Unfortunately, Ramsey Clark never published this important work.)

F**OOD**, A**RT**, M**USIC**, E**NTERTAINMENT**
IN A NEW AGE OF HOTEL HOSPITALITY

WHAT A NAME FOR A HOTEL!

It all adds up to an acronym for what a great hotel should provide:
Food, Art, Music, and Entertainment!

BRANDING THE EVIL OF NUCLEAR BOMB TESTING
(LEADING TO THE ATOMIC TEST BAN TREATY A YEAR LATER)

Nuclear Bomb testing in the atmosphere by the U.S. and Soviet Union was threatening the continuation of life on our planet. In 1962, I designed a poster alerting the public with factual warnings by Nobel scientists that the fallout of radioactive materials would result in a booming number of birth defects. The poster received national attention in the press and on TV. The Committee for Sane Nuclear Testing (SANE), and I, were rewarded for our warnings by being called Communist Sympathizers, and worse – traitors! But Dr. Spock and the Nobel Laureates truly saved the world when their warnings led directly to the historic Atomic Test Ban Treaty of 1963!

GEORGE LOIS, 1962

FAST FORWARDING THE CAREERS OF FILM STUDENTS

To fast forward the careers of film students of today into the world's great film makers of tomorrow, a star-studded panel of industry giants award the most promising, who upload their best student film to fffilmfestival.com and have it seen throughout the world.

fastforward ff.com

WHEN SENATOR WARREN MAGNUSON WAS FIGHTING FOR HIS POLITICAL LIFE, I HAD HIM GIVE HIS OPPONENT THE FINGER

In 1968, getting old and fat and wearing thin after 24 years as a senator, Republicans were certain that Warren Magnuson was finally a cooked goose. So I showed him in a TV spot being ridiculed by a voice-over, finally saying, *So once youth is gone, once dash is gone, what can you possibly offer the voters of Washington?*

He reeled back, gained his composure, and tapped his forehead – once, twice, three times. After the voters saw the senator point a finger and tap his noggin, he became an instant folk hero. An announcer summed it up by saying, *In his rumpled suit, carrying 20 extra pounds, and showing some signs of wear, 'Maggie' remains a giant in the United States Senate.* Branding him Maggie was the finishing touch.

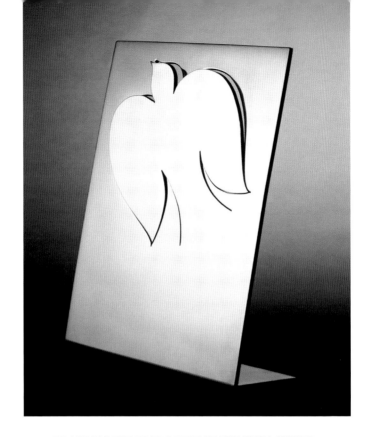

BRANDING THE FREE SPIRIT OF THE YEAR AWARD:
A STRIVING DOVE, TETHERED BUT YEARNING TO BE FREE

In 1992, I was given the honor to design the Al Neuharth Free Spirit of the Year Award for the
Freedom Forum (doing yeomen service protecting freedom of the press).
The award, which comes with $1,000,000 gift, is presented annually to "a courageous achiever
who accomplishes great things beyond his or her normal circumstances."
Fittingly, the first honoree was the journalist Terry Anderson, who had been abducted from the streets
of Beirut and imprisoned for almost seven years, held as a hostage by a group of
Shiite Muslims in Lebanon. Inspired by Picasso's *Dove of Peace*, as well as his breakthrough
sculptural technique of cutting shapes out of a single plane to create forms,
I designed a dove springing out of a sheet of stainless steel. As a newly freed political prisoner,
Anderson was brought to tears holding the award in his arms during
the first presentation dinner in Washington, D.C.

THE 4 GREAT AMERICAN DESIGNERS FOR MEN ARE:

R_____ L_____
P_____ E_____
C_____ K_____
T____ H_____

THIS IS THE LOGO OF THE LEAST KNOWN OF THE FOUR

In most households, the first three names are household words. Get ready to add another. His first name (hint) is Tommy. The second name is not so easy. But in a few short months everybody in America will know there's a new look in town and a new name at the top. Tommy's clothes are easy-going without being too casual, classic without being predictable. He calls them classics with a twist. The other three designers call them competition.

282 Columbus Avenue
at 73rd Street
New York, New York 10023
(212) 877-1270

© 1985 MURJANI

OUTRAGEOUSLY BRANDING THE TOMMY HILFIGER NAME (WITHOUT NAMING HIM!)

This 1985 ad challenged the reader with a wildly audacious claim. Overnight, the burning question in town became "Who the hell is T____ H_____?" Tommy Hilfiger became instantly famous and set off an avalanche of national publicity within days. The ad was a self-fulfilling prophecy because the young, unknown Hilfiger, soon became the most famous and successful designer brand in the world.

PIZZAZZ WITH FIZZ

A store at 73rd Street and Columbus Avenue in Manhattan,
and Paramus Park Mall in New Jersey, exclusively selling Coca-Cola Clothes.
Tommy Hilfiger was hired by Mohan Murjani to design the line.
After meeting Tommy, I really put him on the map with an ad that made him
famous overnight (see previous page).

THE PERFECT NAME FOR A PRODUCT TO KEEP A MAN YOUTHFUL

I named this cologne
Dorian Gray, the most eternally
youthful man in literature.
We avoided any suggestion
of Oscar Wilde
decadence by transforming
him into something
of a dude (with a whiff of
wickedness).
I topped it off with a cap
on the bottle in the
form of the debonair
Dorian's top hat.

Bumble Bee Hydrogen Hybrid

A PRODUCT TO TAKE THE STING OUT OF GAS PRICES

A revolutionary technology that utilizes hydrogen on demand,
reducing fuel consumption by 50%, increasing engine power, lowering emissions,
and saving thousands of dollars in gasoline annually.

"MAKE ME A HALOID XEROX..."
OR "MAKE ME A XEROX!"

XEROX

In 1961, my ad agency, Papert Koenig Lois, was a year old when we were awarded
the Haloid Xerox account. The immediate "no-brainer" was to convince
their honchos to shorten their brand name to Xerox. Joe Wilson and his operating staff
were resistant, even indignant at our suggestion. The process of Xerography
had been conceived in 1938 by Chester Carlson, who offered it to more than 20 major
corporations, among them IBM, General Electric, Eastman Kodak, and RCA.
The abominable No-Men of corporate America turned him down flat. Carlson finally went into
partnership with Haloid, a small, obscure photographic-supply company in
Rochester, and eventually produced the Haloid Xerox 914 copy machine in 1960. But the
word Haloid had to go! After a contentious debate, we won them over, and a
local firm designed a Xerox logo, just in time for our first ads and television commercial.
When our TV spots aired, America went copy crazy—and their 10-year sales
objective was accomplished in six months—and the Xerox culture
(*not* the Haloid Xerox culture) was born.

MAKING THE BRAND NAME *HUE* SOUND LIKE THE WORD *YOU* IN THOUSANDS OF LOVE SONGS

This ad campaign made women sing love songs to Hue legwear and bodywear (designed to fit the rhythm of their life).

YOU ARE MY SPECIAL ANGEL
by Jimmy Duncan (1957)

I ONLY HAVE EYES FOR YOU
Composer, Harry Warren, Lyricist, Al Dubin (1934)

I HONESTLY LOVE YOU
Composer Peter Allen, Lyricist, Jeff Barry (1957)

ALI/FRAZIER III   **NO LOVE LOST**

BRANDING THE FIGHT OF THE CENTURY (THEY JUST DIDN'T LIKE EACH OTHER)

Don King, the Mike Todd and P.T. Barnum of the fight game was promoting the
World Heavyweight Championship rubber match between
Muhammad Ali and Smokin' Joe Frazier — a grudge match played out daily in the press
the world over. I told Don King that there had never been a great
fight program that was so terrific that fight fans would want to save it forever.
So with Harold Hayes as my editor, I designed a powerful,
and hilarious 34-page program, with millions of people at the lucrative closed-circuit
locations receiving them free.

Dave Anderson, the legendary *New York Times* sports reporter, wrote
"There was a great undercard, but none of the reporters watched them — they all had their
faces in a terrific fight program." Two weeks after the bloody fight,
I was gabbing with a cab driver about the stupendous event with the great Ali winning
a TKO in the 14th round. "It was the greatest heavyweight fight I ever saw in
my whole life," the New York hackie said, "almost as good as that program they handed out."

THE NO NONSENSE AMERICAN WOMAN AWARD

The perception of No Nonsense hosiery was that the brand was functional, utilitarian legwear.
Ho, hum. They needed a brand make-over to stop declining market share for
a product found so lackluster. So I created the *No Nonsense American Woman* – the two added
words instantly positioning No Nonsense as a fresh, fashionable brand
that talked sense to the woman of the '90s. The No Nonsense American Woman Award,
announced each month in national magazines, attracted enthusiastic
"testimonials" from Governor Ann Richards of Texas, feminist Gloria Steinem, even Oprah, Liz, Barbra,
and Whoopi, and No Nonsense got a tremendous kick in sales.

TRANSFORMING 87 HARD-SELL CAR SALESMEN INTO CHOIRBOYS

My product imagery satirized the dubious reputation of every car dealer in America by branding them *The Pontiac Choirboys*, and showed them sweetly singing parodies of five folklore melodies, with re-written lyrics. For example, to the tune of *I Surrender Dear*:
You ran away the other day
You said you had one price to pay
Why don't you stop around today
And we'll surrender dear,
followed by a voice-over that whines,
Your Pontiac Dealer
gives up! He'll make any *deal to sell*
you a Pontiac. In unison,
the 87 dealers bring their hands up in a begging gesture.
Car buyers responded, singing our tunes as they drove away in new Pontiacs.

HOW TO MAKE A DULL LOGO SMILE

Ritz Camera Centers sounded snobby and expensive.
But not after America heard: *Say Cheese...with Ritz!* My picture-perfect
four-word slogan in 1996 immediately transformed their logo
and brand imagery into a fun buying experience (always promising service
with a smile) and developed 500 Ritz centers into over 900!

I smoke
Padilla
Hear me roar!

LT. GEN. ANTONIO MACEO WAS THE MOST
COURAGEOUS (AND WOUNDED) GUERILLA LEADER
IN THE TEN YEARS' WAR OF INDEPENDENCE,
KILLED IN ACTION DAYS BEFORE A GLORIOUS VICTORY

*One puff of a Padilla
and you'll roar too.*

BRANDING CIGARS PRODUCED BY THE SONS OF A CUBAN PATRIOT, WITH THE IMAGES OF THE GREATEST HEROES IN CUBA'S FIGHT FOR INDEPENDENCE FROM SPAIN

Heberto Padilla was imprisoned by the Fidel Castro government, but with the support of intellectuals throughout the world, and with the sponsorship of Senator Ted Kennedy, his family, including his two sons, came to America. Living in the land of political freedom, Ernesto and Carlos now proudly blend cigars that continue the magnificent Cuban traditions of cigar making.

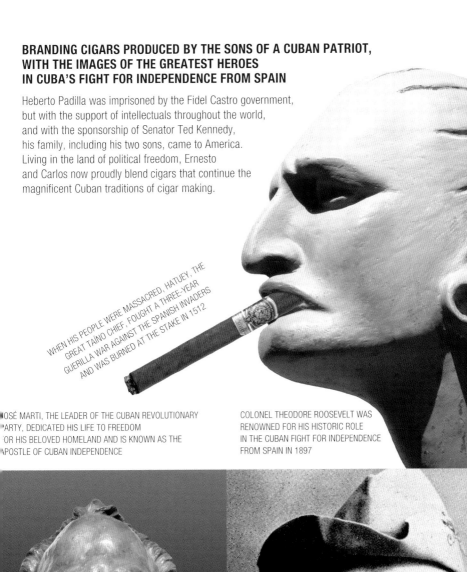

WHEN HIS PEOPLE WERE MASSACRED, HATUEY, THE GREAT TAÍNO CHIEF, FOUGHT A THREE-YEAR GUERILLA WAR AGAINST THE SPANISH INVADERS AND WAS BURNED AT THE STAKE IN 1512

JOSÉ MARTI, THE LEADER OF THE CUBAN REVOLUTIONARY PARTY, DEDICATED HIS LIFE TO FREEDOM FOR HIS BELOVED HOMELAND AND IS KNOWN AS THE APOSTLE OF CUBAN INDEPENDENCE

COLONEL THEODORE ROOSEVELT WAS RENOWNED FOR HIS HISTORIC ROLE IN THE CUBAN FIGHT FOR INDEPENDENCE FROM SPAIN IN 1897

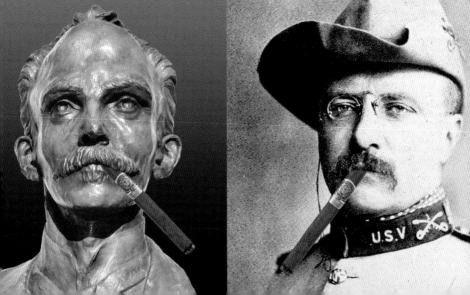

LET'S TWIST AGAIN WITH CHUBBY CHECKER

The '60s were a tumultuous time, culturally, racially, and politically, but the Twist helped define the era. By bridging the generational gap between young and old, men, women, and children everywhere, of every persuasion and background, were twisting. This logo, in 2015, is the beginning of the development of an epic relaunch of Chubby Checker, with new music, a movie and a stage play. (Fifty-five years later, *The Twist* by Chubby Checker is still the *Billboard* Hot 100's All-Time Top Song.)

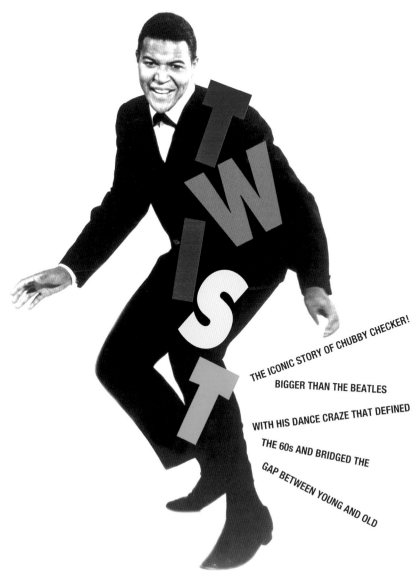

THE ICONIC STORY OF CHUBBY CHECKER!

BIGGER THAN THE BEATLES

WITH HIS DANCE CRAZE THAT DEFINED

THE 60s AND BRIDGED THE

GAP BETWEEN YOUNG AND OLD

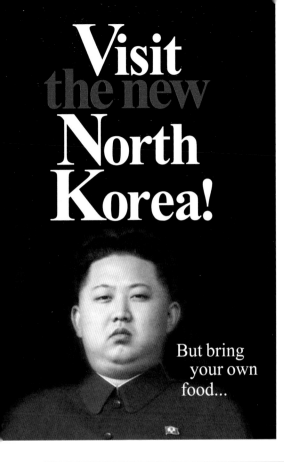

Visit the new North Korea!

But bring your own food...

A SHAM TOURIST POSTER BRANDING KIM JONG-UN'S NEW NORTH KOREA

For Maer Roshan's online magazine *Punch*, my poster winks its eye as it announces a North Korean tourism campaign. The people of North Korea may suffer from the lack of accessible, affordable sustenance, but their Supreme Leader (the son of Kim Jong-il) seems to have grown up in the lap of luxury.

"There was no need to brainwash Romney. All he required was a light rinse."

READ HOW ROBERT SANDOZ
ZAPS THE GOVERNOR IN THIS WEEK'S
NEW LEADER MAGAZINE

BRANDING A CANDIDATE FOR PRESIDENT, "BRAINWASHED"

In 1967, Governor George Romney of Michigan (the father of Mitt Romney), was front-runner for the 1968 Republican Presidential nomination. He was a hawk on Vietnam, but changed his tune during an interview in which he explained that the reason he had ever believed the war was necessary was because he had been "brainwashed" by American generals and diplomats when he made a trip to Saigon in 1965. This tiny ad for the influential weekly, *New Leader*, was the RIP on Romney's political headstone

IDENTIFYING THE FIRST LADY OF THE AESTHETICS
OF MODERNISM IN THE HISTORY OF DESIGN

In 2001, I had the honor to design a cover for *Metropolis* magazine to honor Florence Knoll Basset, the legendary interior space planner and designer. For 80 years now, the name Knoll has been synonymous with superb design of furniture, textiles, and interior planning and design. Florence Knoll battled against a world indifferent to modernism to become an exponent of an extraordinary pantheon of designers, architects, artists, and sculptors who had been associated as creators of work marketed by the Knoll firm: Mies van der Rohe, Eero Saarinen, Harry Bertoia, Marcel Breuer, Isamu Noguchi, Herbert Matter, Alvar Aalto, Jens Risom, and others. Never formerly a teacher, she dynamically taught the world how to live a soulful home and business life of visual pleasure.

the Windex

A DAZZLING SEE-THROUGH LOGO AND SLOGAN, DRIVEN BY THE STIRRING THEME SONG OF *GONE WITH THE WIND*

When the head man of the Windex brand first heard my mantra for his well-known glass and multi-surface cleaner he was blown away.
The gung-ho CEO was almost fired by his bosses at Bristol-Myers because he dearly wanted to give me his ad account (and firing one of the largest ad agencies in the world). So my logo and ad campaign never saw the light of day.

"GEORGE, FIRST I RAP THEM *WITH* MY MOUTH – THEN I RAP THEM *IN* THE MOUTH!"

This book logotype proclaims that Muhammad Ali, as he once told me, was the first heavyweight champion of rap. *Ali Rap* is a book of over 300 rap rhythms, witticisms, insults, wisecracks, politically incorrect quips, courageous stands, and words of inspiration from the mind, heart and soul of the brash young Cassius Clay, as he steadily grew into the magnificent man who is Muhammad Ali.

A PUBLICATION DESIGNED SO THE ICONS LEAP OUT ON A LIBRARY SHELF

In 1972, as president of the New York Art Directors Club, I founded the Art Directors Hall of Fame. The first eight inductees shown on the backbone instead of the traditional title of a book, were pioneering giants of modern design who blazed the trail for the talented art directors and graphic communicators who followed.

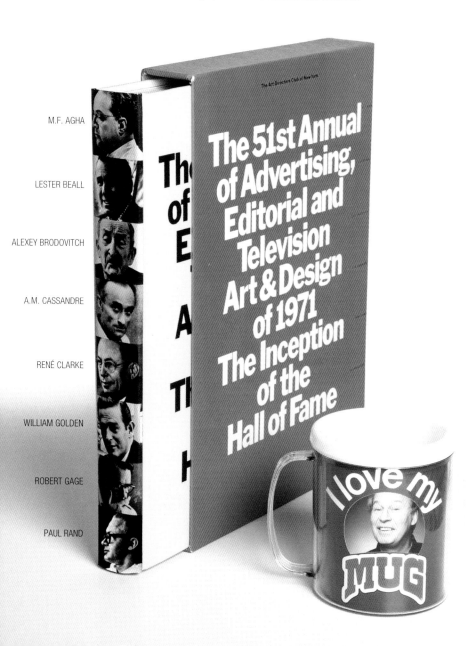

M.F. AGHA

LESTER BEALL

ALEXEY BRODOVITCH

A.M. CASSANDRE

RENÉ CLARKE

WILLIAM GOLDEN

ROBERT GAGE

PAUL RAND

The Art Directors Club of New York

The 51st Annual of Advertising, Editorial and Television Art & Design of 1971 The Inception of the Hall of Fame

TRAV◯LTA FOR MIN◯LTA

A MARRIAGE MADE IN ADVERTISING HEAVEN (BUT IT NEVER HAPPENED)

In 1994, I had a deal in place to enlist John Travolta of *Saturday Night Fever* fame
(and a certified pilot and amateur photographer), to star as the
TV and Print spokesman of the Minolta camera company for an extraordinary low fee.
The charismatic young actor had hit a wall in the early 1990s that
seemed to have derailed his career. A big opportunity for Minolta, I figured.
I could get him for bupkis — and he'd certainly get hot again.
But the obtuse Japanese management team insisted he was not "No. 1"
and they killed my proposed deal. Six months later,
Pulp Fiction premiered and Travolta was bigger than ever.

A GIRL CAN NEVER HAVE ENOUGH SOCKS APPEAL!

BY K. BELL

In 1990, Karen Bell, a talented designer,
socked it to the fashion industry
with her single-minded love of designing
socks for women (and only socks),
with imagination and exuberant style.

I LOVE MY MUG (ROOT BEER!)

For Pepsi, to change an old fashioned, turn-of-the-19th century beverage into a modern,
popular, mass-appeal drink, I transformed their brand name, Mug, into
a double entendre. Richard "Jaws" Kiel, the dark-toothed villain of James Bond 007 films,
and the outrageous Phyllis Diller (whose mug changed each year) helped
make Mug the number one root beer in New York. This promotional cup, where your
photo could be inserted in place, became a popular promotional item.
(My mug graces this mug.)

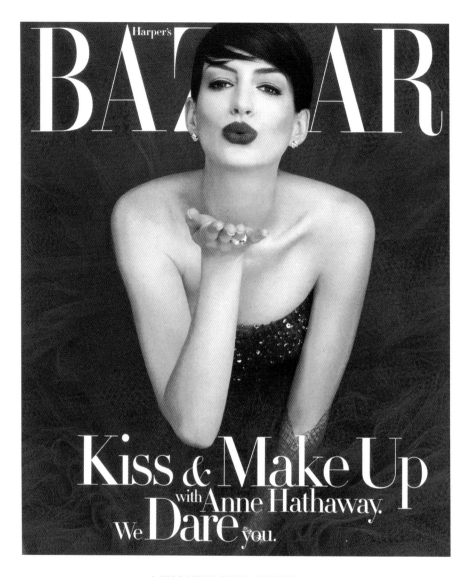

Harper's

BAZAAR

Kiss & Make Up
with Anne Hathaway.
We Dare you.

A MAGAZINE COVER KISSING OFF
THE SICKOFANS WHO BRANDED THEMSELVES HATHAHATERS

I was asked by Glenda Bailey, *Harper Bazaar*'s super-editor, how I would handle doing
a feature story and cover on the daring and talented Anne Hathaway,
who was upset and troubled over the unfair treatment she had been receiving
over a minor flub when she was awarded her Oscar for her brilliant
portrayal of Fantine in *Les Misérables*. At a meeting at Harper's, I told the anxious young
actress, "Don't get mad, just kiss and make up." And she did.

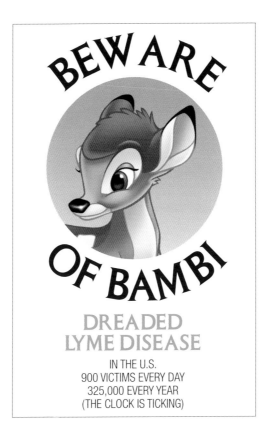

A FUNNY (BUT DEADLY SERIOUS LOGO)

A logo warning of the dreaded Lyme disease caused by the bite of an infected deer tick.
Every tick of the clock brings a life-threatening chronic illness to an unsuspecting
American. The double entendre of the sound of a clock tick, tick, ticking – and millions
of ticks bite, bite, biting, infecting 900 victims every day, is a chilling
and incredibly memorable brand name for a Research Center dedicated to finding
a cure to the devastating disease.

DON'T GOOGLE IT–GIVADAMN!

Givadamn.com – a brand name for a damn good website offering tens
of thousands of creative and inspirational items and concepts
to promote a company's brand, as well as excite their customers.

MANE

*It's good
to be
the King!*

FAME<small>NYC</small>™

We style manes
for famous names.
Come on in.

IN TODAY'S CULTURE, FAME IS THE NAME OF THE GAME

For over 20 years, Steve Vilot, the Master Barber in America,
owner of three barbershops and a legendary figure to the nations' top barbers,
developed ground-breaking, on-site barbering to famous celebrities,
athletes, and rock stars. To build a cutting edge national business, I branded
his venture Mane Fame, with a unique selling proposition to millions
of American men who want to look cool: *We style manes for famous names.*

A WACKY NAME FOR A CABLE COMPANY

In the early 1990s, Warner-Amex Communications Inc. had a severe public image perception, with a tremendous "churn" of their cable TV subscribers. They were badly in need of a campaign to help change their image. I convinced the suits at Warner-Amex to change their brand name by adopting their initials, which phonetically read *wacky*. "(City name) is going WACCI" almost immediately won over TV viewers in trouble spots all over America.

WARNER-AMEX CABLE COMMUNICATIONS INC.

traválo

NEVER TRAVÁLO WITHOUT ONE!

Traválo is a refillable perfume container that *Elle* magazine called "The most genius beauty gadget, ever!"and *Vogue* wrote, "It's amazing!!! Magically it's full. Don't travel anywhere without it." Women merely refill directly from their favorite fragrance bottle, in seconds, with no possibility of spills or leaks. To communicate the correct pronunciation of Traválo, I created the stylish one above that emphasizes "vá."

vá

THE REFILLABLE PERFUME CONTAINER FOR WOMEN ON THE GO!

Sitting in the middle of my new Traválo logo, I spotted the perfect brand name for a luxury line of the patented, refillable perfume container: "vá!" (which means "go" in multiple languages).

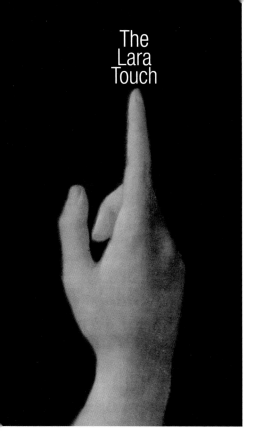

The Lara Touch

GET IN TOUCH WITH YOUR LIFE WITH THE LARA TOUCH

Lara Licharowicz is a former professional dancer turned fitness trainer who struggled with chronic fatigue syndrome prior to discovering Eden Energy medicine. In just 15 minutes a day, her revolutionary Lara Touch can boost your overall energy and decrease your body's reaction to stress (and drop two jean sizes).

BEEFEATER GIN & A JUICY NEW YORK STRIP STEAK

A Beefeater promotion that synergistically brands one of the world's best gins, with the enjoyment of gripping a steak knife with a Beefeater logo, and the name of the steakhouse on the blade – and slicing away.

STOP!

A name and logo that powerfully warns the bad guys (and tech-savvy, young music fans) that piracy of video entertainment, with the use of a new coding and tracking system, *will* be stopped!

BRANDING REVLON'S MILK-PLUS SIX SHAMPOO WITH A COW

In 1974, to launch Revlon's innovative shampoo, I showed model Susan Blakely, standing in a lovely meadow, as she sweetly said, *Like my hair? Meet my hairdresser*, as the scene widened to reveal a cow as it delivered a mellifluous *Mooooo*!

Hairdressers all over America (I'm not kidding) actually mooooooed as they shampooed women's hair with Milk-Plus Six for over a decade.

"Mooooo!"

BRANDING A DAMN GOOD BOOK
(IN SEVEN LANGUAGES)

Damn Good Advice is the culmination of my
lifetime of iconoclastic thinking and
teaching about the process of creativity:
120 no-holds barred, in-your-face
lessons explaining, demonstrating, and
ultimately teaching how to
unleash your potential in any
creatively-driven industry.
If you have no talent, don't buy this book
(no matter what language it's in).

DAMN GOOD ADVICE
(for people with talent!)
How to Unleash Your Creative Potential
by America's Master Communicator
George Lois

PHAIDON

ΕΞΩ ΑΠΟ ΤΑ ΔΟΝΤΙΑ
(συμβουλές για ανθρώπους με ταλέντο!)
Ο Ελληνοαμερικανός Γκουρού της Διαφήμισης
σε Βοηθάει να Απογειώσεις τη Δημιουργικότητά σου.
George Lois

SACRÉS BONS CONSEILS
(for people with talent!)
Comment débrider votre potentiel créatif
par le maître américain de la communication
George Lois

PHAIDON

ON THIS PAGE:
ENGLISH, GREEK, AND
FRENCH EDITIONS

VERDAMMT GUTE TIPPS
(für Leute mit Talent!)
Entdecke Dein kreatives Potenzial
mit Amerikas Kommunikationsgenie
George Lois

PHAIDON

¡QUÉ BUEN CONSEJO!
(para gente con talento)
Cómo liberar tu potencial creativo,
por el gran maestro de la comunicación
George Lois

OCEANO

ON

OLAĞAN ÜSTÜ TAVSİYELER
(yetenekli kişiler için!)
İçinizdeki Yaratıcı Potansiyeli
Ortaya Çıkarmanın 120 Yolu
George Lois

By
BOYNER YAYINLARI

MINDBLOWER

HERO

THE ABOVE AND BEYOND ELECTRIC VEHICLE FROM BARHAM MOTORS

THESE DAYS, WE ALL NEED A HERO

Naming any product Hero would seem to be the height of braggadocio. What manner of product could ever be created that could earn such an accolade? Oliver Wendall Holmes once said, "To think great thoughts you must be a hero as well as an idealist." Surprisingly, and unabashedly, the achievement of the electric vehicle envisioned by Isaac Barham and his brilliant technological and business team can be regarded, and memorably expressed, as a Hero of our time: a totally innovative, culture-busting, safety-oriented, energy-saving, all-American Hero that is going to electrify the family car industry.

GOT A MINDBLOWING IDEA?
GO TO MINDBLOWER.CO AND
LIGHT THE FUSE

In 2015, concentrating on the superb design schools throughout the world, a website addressed to inventors and entrepreneurs to powerfully bring their ideas to marketplace.

SWISH-H-H!

In 1997, hundreds of retired NBA players organized to work to help old-timers who had been denied retirement benefits. They named themselves: the National Retired Basketball Players Association. A-a-a-air ball! I changed their name, memorably, to XNBA.

A TRIBUTE TO THE 500 WHO BUILT THE NBA INTO THE PINNACLE OF SPORTS

In 1998, New York Knicks' great Dave DeBusschere and I organized an XNBA Awards Gala at the New York Hilton, honoring the greatest players in NBA history, men who played their hearts out long before athletes received their fair share of professional sports revenue.

The monumental X Award I designed was presented to 35 iconic NBA legends. (Muhammad Ali was one of the presenters.) The dinner provided assistance and scholarship aid to 500 retired players, and helped forge a much improved NBA pension plan. Commissioner David Stern called the night "The most memorable and emotional gathering in the history of the NBA."

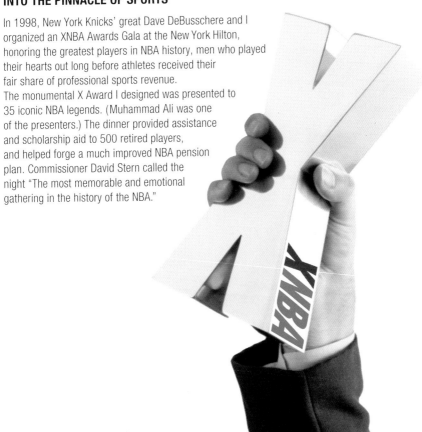

G come home to
Greece
where it all began!

BRANDING A NATION:
NON-GREEKS TELL AMERICA THEY WERE
"GOING HOME...TO GREECE!"

In 1985, following a hijacking at the Athens Airport,
President Reagan warned Americans *not* to travel to Greece.
Planes carrying tourists stopped mid-air!
So I recruited 39 celebs (of non-Greek lineage) to tell America
that *they* were going home...to Greece!
As a proud Greek-American, to contain this terminal damage
to tourism to Greece, the birthplace of democracy,
"where it all began," my commercials demonstrated how Greece
was fighting terrorism by dramatizing how famous
Americans would not kowtow to terrorists. Olympic and TWA flights
filled to capacity and the Greek economy enjoyed a landslide
tourist season – its most glorious ever.

MAKE
TIME
FOR
TIME

NOW MORE THAN EVER,
MAKE TIME FOR TIME

In 1989, a four word slogan
with the product name used twice!
Make time for Time was a call
to action that infused the newsweekly
with a new relevance as their
readers were abandoning them under
the pressures of the information
explosion. Subscriptions jumped 20%
and newsstand sales 22%.

LLOYD BRIDGES

Mama used to tell me that my ancestors
from the British Isles came over
on the Mayflower. Now I'm going home...
to Greece.

SHECKY GREENE

My mother vas coming from
Russia to this vunderful America.
Now I'm going home...
to Greece.

ZSA ZSA GABOR

I was born in Hungary.
Now, darling, I'm finally going home...
to Greece.

NEIL SEDAKA

My grandparents left Poland
and Russia and came to Brooklyn.
Now, at last, I'm going home...
to Greece.

RODDY McDOWALL

I was born in London and came
to America when I was 12 years old.
Now, at last, I'm going home...
to Greece.

BRANDING ALLEN DULLES AS A DEVIL IN AN EPIC BATTLE FOR AMERICA'S SOUL

During a decade-long reign as America's intelligence chief, from 1953-1961, Allen Dulles turned the CIA into the most powerful colossus in Washington. David Talbot's chilling book reveals an unseen world of power, espionage, and violence, masterminded by CIA czar Allen Dulles, the devil incarnate. Presidents came and went, but his power grinded relentlessly forward. When John F. Kennedy was intent on easing the Cold War, the author shows, step-by-step, how Dulles was instrumental in the assassination of our young president.

THE DEVIL'S CHESSBOARD

Allen Dulles,
the Secret Government
and the
Death of the Kennedys
David Talbot

A lot of media people are saying USA TODAY is neither fish nor fowl.

They're right!

THE ADVERTISING MIGHT OF

USA TODAY

To our readers, we're a newspaper-bold, exciting, colorful and unique. To many of our advertisers, we're a newsmagazine—bold, exciting, colorful and unique. The truth is, we don't much care what you call us. Just as long as you call us.

Call Valerie Salembier at (212) 715-5380

THE WISDOM OF A NEGATIVE VISUAL BRANDING OF AN INNOVATIVE NEWSPAPER MADISON AVENUE REFUSED TO ADVERTISE IN

One of the most important innovations in modern journalism was the creation in 1982 of the first national newspaper, *USA Today*. Readers took to it immediately, but advertisers stayed away in droves. So I created this ad that tackled the question of *USA Today*'s identity head on: the burning doubts media buyers had was whether it was a newspaper or a news magazine. So I branded *USA Today* as a freak of nature with a body of a rooster and the tail of a fish, and wrote, *A lot of media people are saying USA Today is neither fish nor fowl. They're right! The truth is…we don't care what you call us, so long as you call us.* And they called us! In no time, they went from selling 2 pages of advertising per issue to 28.

SIGNATURE MAGAZINE WOULDN'T LET ME REDESIGN THEIR LOGO, BUT MY AD CAMPAIGN BROUGHT THEIR BRAND NAME TO LIFE

My copy in each ad sold the power of Citicorp Publishing, a financial institution. What some signatures stand for is very clear, even if the handwriting isn't. They visualize ambition, success, genius and courage. There's another signature that stands for power. Executive power, intellectual power, buying power. That power is in *Signature* magazine.

Throughout History, there's been power in a signature.

GEORGE III

GEORGE WASHINGTON

NAPOLEON

HO CHI MINH

RICHARD III

CHARLES V

THEODORE ROOSEVELT

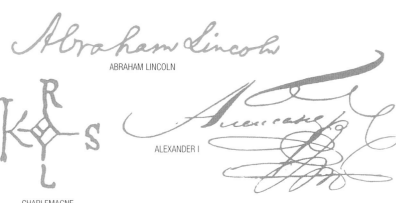

ABRAHAM LINCOLN

ALEXANDER I

CHARLEMAGNE

ANDREW JACKSON

ELIZABETH I

PETER THE GREAT

WINSTON CHURCHILL

There still is.

POISON GAS FILM

Films that bring
tears to your eyes,
unhinge your nervous system,
and knock you out.

THE (COUGH, COUGH) NAME OF A FILM COMPANY PRODUCING A DOCUMENTARY ON ME

The name was inspired by an outrageous remark I made on the David Suskind TV show in the early 1970s, in an interview with me and two CEOs of giant ad agencies. "Gentlemen, what is advertising?," Suskind asked. As I listened to the two advertising stiffs, the camera spotted me and Suskind said, "Why are you making faces, George – what do *you* think advertising is?" "Advertising," I replied, "is poison gas. It should bring tears to your eyes, unhinge your nervous system, and knock you out."

LOOK FOR THE FLOUR WITH THE BOY ON THE BAG

In a day when more and more companies unwisely reject a charming, wordless logo that had originally made them famous, I spotted the 19th century logo on the wall in the office of the president of Heckers Flour in Kansas City, re-drew the boy, and made the kid, cutting a loaf of bread, the star of the flour section. Atta boy!

BE AFRAID. BE VERY AFRAID.

A name and logo for a proposed international TV network relentlessly playing the scariest classic and contemporary horror movies ever made: *Nosferatu, The Shining, Dead of Night, Halloween, The Fly, The Exorcist, The Texas Chainsaw Massacre...* everything to keep you up all night and scare the shit out of you.

BOO-TV

"I'M SO EXCITED ABOUT MY DON KING BOXING CHANNEL, IT MAKES MY HAIR STAND ON END"

Don King (the Mike Todd and P.T. Barnum of the fight game) failed to fulfill his dream of his own TV channel, with a mix of live title bouts, classic fights and original programming. Which only goes to prove, you can't win 'em all.

DON KING TV

BRANDING A RESIDENCE WITH 24 TEARFUL CHORDS

The Butterfield House, my residence for over 50 years in Greenwich Village, is one of the most architecturally significant and beautiful post-WWII apartment houses in New York City, named after Union General Daniel Butterfield, the composer of *Taps*. This poster graces the hallway, in memory of the general's contribution to all who have been sacrificed in our noble, and a few ignoble, adventures.

BRANDING THE EMPOWERMENT OF THE MOBILE SENIOR

Nearly two million seniors are treated for falls each year because of the lack of a safe and stable mobility aid. To come to their aid, Chris Crowley, a geriatric care expert, conceived the Strider, a revolutionary mobility aid and shopping cart that keeps seniors moving in comfort, safety, and style. I branded it The Billy Jean King Strider, after the great tennis champion and iconic fighter for gender equality and proponent of health benefits for the intrepid seniors of the world.

UNION GENERAL DANIEL BUTTERFIELD, COMPOSER OF *TAPS*, WHICH WAS SOUNDED BY BUGLERS IN BOTH THE UNION AND CONFEDERATE ARMIES, AND REMAINED THE MOST POIGNANT MUSICAL CHORDS IN AMERICAN HISTORY

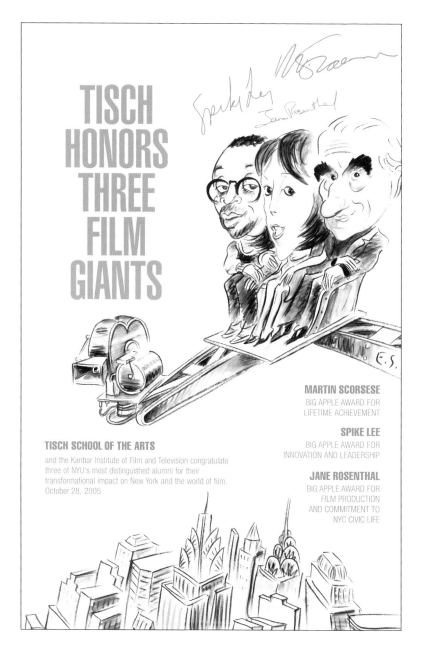

TISCH
HONORS
THREE
FILM
GIANTS

MARTIN SCORSESE
BIG APPLE AWARD FOR
LIFETIME ACHIEVEMENT

SPIKE LEE
BIG APPLE AWARD FOR
INNOVATION AND LEADERSHIP

TISCH SCHOOL OF THE ARTS
and the Kanbar Institute of Film and Television congratulate
three of NYU's most distinguished alumni for their
transformational impact on New York and the world of film.
October 28, 2005

JANE ROSENTHAL
BIG APPLE AWARD FOR
FILM PRODUCTION
AND COMMITMENT TO
NYC CIVIC LIFE

BRANDING THE TISCH SCHOOL OF THE ARTS WITH THREE FILM GIANTS

In 2005, the best film school in the U.S. honored Martin Scorsese, Spike Lee,
and Jane Rosenthal (three of NYU's most distinguished alumni),
with their Big Apple Awards. I asked the great illustrator, Edward Sorel, to depict
our three magnificent fellow New Yorkers high above the skyline,
looking down upon our beloved city.

**DEMOCRATIC &
REPUBLICAN
PRESIDENTIAL
CONVENTION**
NEWS FROM CBS TELEVISION
PRESS INFORMATION ⓒ 485
MADISON AVENUE NEW YORK

"THRU THE PERILOUS FIGHT...
GAVE PROOF THROUGH THE NIGHT
THAT OUR FLAG WAS STILL THERE"

In 1952, a few weeks after I returned from the war in Korea, Bill Golden, the corporate design pioneer who created the CBS Television graphic style, assigned me to design a logotype and letterhead for the CBS coverage of the upcoming Democratic and Republican Presidential Conventions. There have been dozens of flag rip-offs of my design since, but in 1952, this one created a helluva flap.

Senator Joseph McCarthy attacked CBS for "desecrating our flag," the House Un-American Activities Committee denounced CBS for "un-Americanism," and, already under attack in those terrible days of McCarthyism, the CBS honchos flinched. Bill Golden warned me there could be a decision one night to kill my flag letterhead to placate the Red-baiters. Early the next morning, Golden informed me that the courageous CBS brass finally decided, "To hell with McCarthy and his gang."

FOR BRANIFF INTERNATIONAL: BRANDING
A COMPETITIVE AIRLINE AS DULL AND UNEVENTFUL

In 1967, Braniff International was flying half-full from New York to Dallas (their home base). American Airlines totally dominated the route and seemed unbeatable. So I created a zany, wildly outrageous ad campaign that featured a smorgasbord of the world's oddest couples, exchanging the screwiest and most sophisticated chatter ever heard on television, all ending with the battle cry delivered by the celeb that gained the upside in a repartee with his fellow passenger with *When you got it – Flaunt it!* My juxtaposition of celebrities created the perception that when you flew Braniff, you never knew who might be in the seat next to you. I filmed seven celebrity odd couples, including Andy Warhol talking to a catatonic Sonny Liston (below) trying to out-bullshit each other as they fly Braniff. Within a week of running the campaign, Braniff became the hot ticket in the route between New York and Dallas/Ft. Worth, and the planes filled to capacity with star-gazers. *When you got it – Flaunt it!* became an American colloquialism as well as a standard entry in the anthologies of American sayings, almost instantly.

"When you got it –
Flaunt it!"

"Wheeee, Pirelli!"

IN 1974, MOST AMERICANS
THOUGHT PIRELLI
WAS A BRAND OF SPAGHETTI

Pirelli is an Italian steel-belted radial tire,
whose advertising in America had always hidden the fact that they were Italian.
As far as I was concerned, a tire with Italian origin was part of that country's great racing
and car design tradition. So I enlisted a high-fashion model with the lyrical name
Appolonia. She spoke with a voluptuous northern Italian brogue, sensually rolling the name
Pirelli on her sophisticated tongue, always caressing a tire or two, even swinging in one.
On viewing my campaign of eight TV spots, thousands of Tommaso, Dick and Harry's said
arrivederci to Firestone, Goodyear and Goodrich and switched to Pirelli,
the molto fantastico tire. Capish?

"Ever since I became the first lady jockey, I ride Braniff." (When you got it – Flaunt it.)

BRANDING THE COMING OF THE AGE OF WOMEN ATHLETES SPARKING THE FEMINIST MOVEMENT

Sure, there was Babe Didrikson Zaharias, superb in golf, basketball, and track and field – but in 1969, Diane Crump, America's first female jockey, went mano a mano with the most competitive and nastiest male athletes in sports. Requiring a full police escort, Crump described her first race, "The hecklers were yelling, 'Go back to the kitchen and cook dinner!' They thought I was going to be the downfall of the whole sport – come on people, this is the 1960s!" She went on to ride 235 wins.

AND IN 1973, PREDICTING THE COMING OF THE GREAT BILLIE JEAN KING

As part of a newspaper ad campaign for Cutty Sark that commented on newsworthy happenings, I ran this ad the morning after the outspoken 55 year-old male chauvinist Bobby Riggs, humiliated Australian tennis ace Margaret Court Smith in a $50,000 winner-take-all match. Four months later, Billie Jean King destroyed Bobby Riggs in *The Battle of the Sexes*, winning $100,000 and the respect of men and women worldwide.

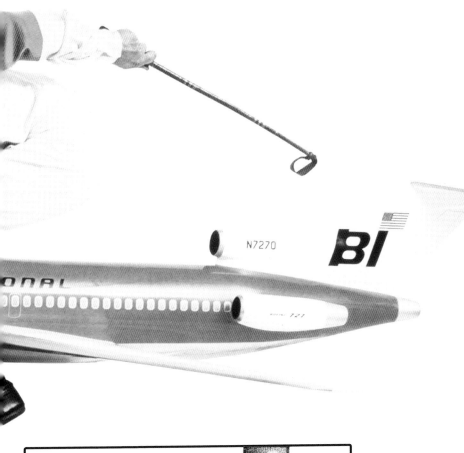

INTER·CONTINENTAL,
AGAIN AND AGAIN.

INTER·CONTINENTAL,
ENCORE ET ENCORE.

INTER·CONTINENTAL,
WIEDER UND WEIDER.

WHEN YOU CREATE A GREAT BRANDING SLOGAN, REPEAT IT AGAIN AND AGAIN

InterContinental Hotels had a low awareness with business travelers, but those that stayed
at one of their hotels returned, again and again. So in the TV commercials
we filmed in eight of their locations all over the world, I had each general manager exclaim,
Welcome to InterContinental, Again and Again. Their logo was weak and
undistinguished, so they allowed me to design a new one. I had each hotel adapt my logo,
followed by "Again and Again" (in the language of their location)
on their letterhead, promotional material and advertising. Awareness of InterContinental
went through the roof as bookings increased over 50%,
and the majority of their new guests became repeat customers (again and again).

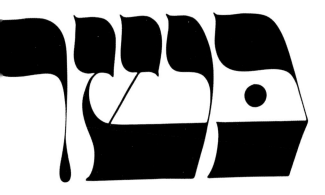

REBRANDING A PRODUCT...IN HEBREW!

In 1959, for a Goodman's Matzos New York subway poster, I showed a giant matzoh and under it a Goodman's package with the subhead *in the best Passover tradition!*
Over the huge matzoh, I hand-lettered the headline, in Hebrew, that proudly proclaimed *Kosher for Passover*. The poster stopped subway riders in their tracks – Jews and gentiles alike, and established Goodman's, not Manischewitz, not Streit's, not Yehuda, as the authentic Hebrew matzoh – all from a Greek Orthodox atheist.

WHY DID HE FOLLOW MARTIN, A POLICE OFFICER ASKED.
"THESE ASSHOLES, THEY ALWAYS GET AWAY," ZIMMERMAN ANSWERED.

What is most frightening is that there are so many people with guns in America like George Zimmerman
a self-appointed vigilante posing as a protector against "fucking punks." Fear and racism
may never be fully eliminated by legislative or judicial order, but neither should Florida's Self-Defense,
Stand Your Ground laws facilitate the murder of an unarmed 17 year-old African-American
walking home from a convenience store. This page I created for *The Nation* magazine in 2012 brands
Zimmerman's murder of Trayvon Martin as a vicious act of racism.

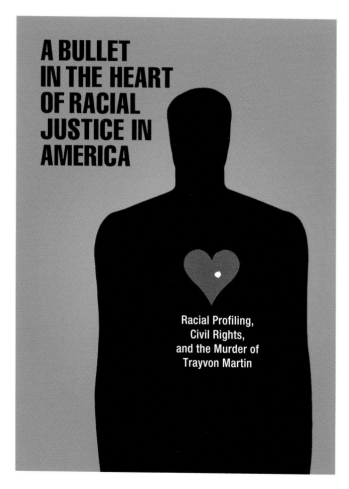

LAW ENFORCERS (WHOSE STANDARD OPERATING PROCEDURE
IS TO STOP A SUSPECTED PERPETRATOR, RATHER THAN AIM TO KILL),
PRACTICE ON THIS TARGET SILHOUETTE OF A HUMAN BEING.

Without political satire, we are all enslaved.

Merci Beaucoup, Charlie Hebdo

George Lois

CONTROVERSIAL, YES

But when asked by *Vice* magazine for my reaction to a 2015 terrorist attack
on *Charlie Hebdo*, the French satirical weekly news magazine,
in response to a controversial Muhammad cartoon it published – I gave tribute,
not to the cartoon, but their courage, and right, to print it.

Reebok

Pump up
and Air out!

SALES SOARED FROM $100 MILLION TO HALF A BILLION
WHEN I SHOWED ATHLETES SWISHING AIR JORDAN'S INTO A GARBAGE CAN

In 1990, Reebok Pump technology was seen as gimmicky,
until I put the words *Pump up and Air out* on the lips of trash-talker Dominique Wilkins,
who dissed Michael Jordan (and Nike) by exclaiming,
Michael my man, if you want to fly first class...Pump up and air out!, and then took
a smooth 15-foot foul shot, swishing an Air Jordan into
a wastebasket. I followed up my non-stop TV assault with five more superstar athletes:
Greg Norman, Dennis Rodman, Michael Chang, Boomer Esiason,
and Dave Johnson, all lobbing Air Jordan's into the garbage. We ran the Dominique and
Boomer spots during the 1991 Super Bowl game and
sales rocketed, with Reebok stock vaulting from $10 a share to $35.

They used to call us "McPaper"...

"USA TODAY
is hot...
From the start,
it has been criticized
by some purists as
'fast-food journalism,'
but its use of
color and graphics
have clearly
made an impact
on newspapers
nationwide."
NEWSDAY
SEPTEMBER 4, 1986

now they call us No.1!

REBRANDING THE MOST MALIGNED (GREAT) NEWSPAPER IN THE USA

One of the most important innovations in modern journalism was the creation in 1983 of the first
national newspaper, *USA Today*. It was the brainchild of Gannett's gutsy chairman,
Al Neuharth, and readers took to it immediately, but advertisers stayed away in droves.
A year later, it had a circulation of over 1.1 million, making it the third largest
daily newspaper in the country. But so-called media critics in America derisively nicknamed
Neuharth's pride and joy, "McPaper," insinuating, hell, condemning it,
as fast-food journalism. But as *USA Today*'s circulation grew, advertisers still wouldn't bite.
Somehow I had to put an end to the insult, if only to keep the great Al Neuharth
from going bonkers whenever he heard the dreaded nickname. The day I was told that
USA Today's circulation was #1 in the nation, I destroyed any possible
McPaper bad-mouthing with the simple statement,
They used to call us McPaper, now they call us No.1!

See it Now presents Edward R. Murrow

A REPORT ON SENATOR JOE McCARTHY

CBS

Tonight 9:00pm

DEPICTING EDWARD R. MURROW AS THE SLAYER OF McCARTHYISM

CBS Television scheduled a stinging indictment on March 9, 1954 of Senator Joseph McCarthy and the shameful period of McCarthyism that gripped the very soul of America. I was a 23-year-old Korean War vet who was thrilled to be a designer in Bill Golden's "Corporate Image" design department, when he had the courage to give blacklisting victim Ben Shahn the assignment to do a satirical drawing of McCarthy for a tune-in ad. So I, outrageously, asked Ben Shahn to do a drawing of Edward R. Murrow spearing Joe McCarthy as an evil dragon. A few days later Shahn proudly handed me his revengeful, yet heroic drawing. The imagery exploded in the morning newspapers and McCarthyism was dead, even before the show ran that night.

BRANDING GREECE'S ECONOMIC PLIGHT IN A TEDx TALK
BY SAYING NO TO FASCISM, THEN, AND NOW

Every October 28 in Greece is OXI Day, commemorating the answer the Greek
Prime Minister gave to Mussolini in 1940, when the fascist leader gave
Greece an ultimatum to allow Axis forces to invade Greece. I resurrected that heroic
incident in a 2014 TEDx talk to an intrepid audience of young Greeks.

My talk ended with this clarion call:
"Say OXI to Fascism, then, and now!
Say OXI to racism, anti-semitism, and homophobia.
Say OXI to tax cheats who threaten the future of Greece.
Say OXI to government that benefits the wealthy at the expense of the poor and powerless.
Say YES every October 28, and be proud of your heritage."

There wasn't a dry eye in the audience.

THE BRANDING OF A TUMULTUOUS AMERICAN DECADE

The 1960s had been a decade of titanic crusades, as protests and marches advanced the fight for Civil Rights, and Women's Liberation, as the Vietnam War and its atrocities escalated, culminating after the 1962 assassination of President John F. Kennedy, with the excruciating assassinations in 1968 of Dr. Martin Luther King and Senator Robert F. Kennedy in the span of 9 weeks.

Month after month, the covers helped define that period as the Golden Age of Journalism in American history. Now seen as a collection of a representative showing of *Esquire* covers, 35 of them are installed in the permanent collection of the Museum of Modern art, branding, nailing and impaling America's most chaotic decade, and as MoMA has stated, have become essential to the iconography of American Culture.

MY FIRST ESQUIRE COVER OUTRAGEOUSLY PREDICTED, AND DEPICTED, THAT SONNY LISTON, AN 8-TO-1 UNDERDOG, WOULD KO CHAMPION FLOYD PATTERSON (INCLUDING THE COLOR OF THIS TRUNKS).

CASSIUS CLAY ON SONNY LISTON
AS SANTA CLAUS:
"THE LAST BLACK MOTHERFUCKER
AMERICA WANTS TO SEE
COMING DOWN *THEIR* CHIMNEY!"

A NATION'S TEARS:
THE MURDER OF OUR PRESIDENT
WAS AN UNRELIEVED TRAUMA,
BREAKING THE HEARTS
AND DASHING THE HOPES OF
A NEW GENERATION.

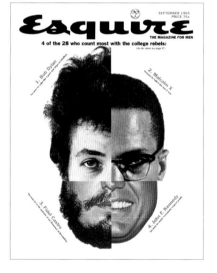

A PREMATURE INDICTMENT
OF VIETNAM BECOMING A WAR OF
GENOCIDE. THE WORDS ARE
THOSE OF A GI, TWO YEARS BEFORE
THE MY LAI MASSACRE.

THE FACE OF A HERO THAT
INFURIATED AMERICA: IN 1965,
THE YOUTH OF AMERICA
CHOSE BOB DYLAN, MALCOLM X,
FIDEL CASTRO, AND JFK AS
THEIR REVOLUTIONARY HEROES.

AN ALL-AMERICAN KID WATCHING
JACK RUBY SHOOT LEE HARVEY OSWALD
DEAD, LIVE ON TV, DEPRIVING
AMERICA OF LEARNING THE FULL TRUTH
ABOUT THE ASSASSINATION OF JFK.

BRANDING MUHAMMAD ALI AS A
MARTYR FOR REFUSING TO
FIGHT IN A BAD WAR: COMBINING
RACE, RELIGION AND THE
VIETNAM WAR IN ONE ICONIC IMAGE.

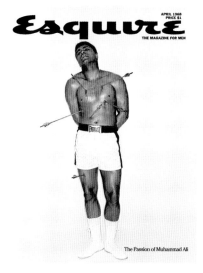

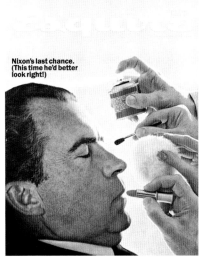

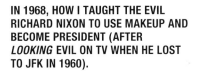

IN 1968, HOW I TAUGHT THE EVIL
RICHARD NIXON TO USE MAKEUP AND
BECOME PRESIDENT (AFTER
LOOKING EVIL ON TV WHEN HE LOST
TO JFK IN 1960).

APOTHEOSIS! PAYING HOMAGE
TO JOHN KENNEDY, ROBERT KENNEDY
AND DR. KING, IN A DREAMLIKE
EPITAPH ON THE MURDER OF
AMERICAN GOODNESS.

ANDY WARHOL BEING DEVOURED
BY FAME: THE JUXTAPOSITION OF THE
CELEBRATION OF POP CULTURE...
AS IT DECONSTRUCTED CELEBRITY.

BRANDING THE COPS OF AMERICA!
THROUGHOUT THOSE NASTY YEARS,
ANTI-WAR DEMONSTRATORS WERE
MET WITH DERISION AND POLICE
VIOLENCE (YOU SHOULDA HEARD
THE COPS SQUEAL).

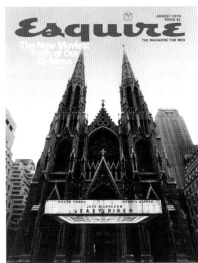

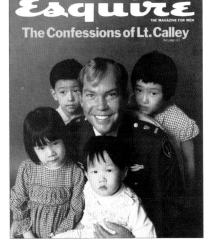

A MARQUE TOUTING *EASY RIDER*
OVER THE MAJESTIC DOORS
OF ST. PATRICK'S CATHEDRAL
(THE ARCHDIOCESE OF NEW YORK
WAS NOT PLEASED).

BRANDING LT. CALLEY AS A KILLER OF
OLD MEN, WOMEN AND CHILDREN:
A GRINNING, CACKLING WAR CRIMINAL
AWAITING TRIAL FOR HIS ROLE
IN THE MY LAI MASSACRE.

LOOKING UP AT THE PROVERBIAL "GLASS CEILING:" BRANDING THE CULMINATION OF THE WOMAN'S MOVEMENT IN AMERICAN POLITICS (SO FAR)

In the year 2000, when the clubby male bastion of the 107th Senate was invaded by a record number of 13 females. Tina Brown was then the editor of *Talk* magazine. We knew what a coup it would be to record this historic event, and photographer Jason Schmidt and I knew we would only get a few minutes with the senators on the first day of their new term. After swiftly composing them from a 20-foot ladder, shooting through a precarious chandelier, Barbara Mikulsky, the senate's 4'11" dynamo, blurted out:

"My neck hurts. Posing like this feels stupid.
 What are we supposed to be looking at? Get the damn camera
 down here and shoot it straight!" I yelled down,
"Ladies, you're all looking up at the proverbial glass ceiling!"
 They burst out laughing and each one nailed
 the camera with devastating charm.

Perhaps, by being elected president, Senator Hillary Clinton
(shown top left) will fulfill Susan B. Anthony's lifetime ambition
for the women of America when she proclaimed, "Oh,
if I could but live another century and see the fruition of all the
work for women! There is so much yet to be done."

THE SUSAN B. ANTHONY
DOLLAR

Weep for Greece.

Poor betrayed Greece.
Dead speech.
Dead press.
Dead liberty.

The silence makes it worse.
Greece is so quiet today, that it's easy to forget.
Across that gentle land, a wicked government demands
allegiance, exacts obedience, destroys opposition.
The list of political prisoners grows every day.
The torture of "traitors" is refined, hour by hour.

To: North American Greek Relief Fund.
% St. Peter's Episcopal Church
346 West 20th Street
New York City, 10011

I can afford $_____
I enclose my check for that amount.
This is how we distribute contributions:
$28.50 per month to families of political prisoners.
$42.30 per month to large families.
$14.10 per month to relatives living alone.

NAME
ADDRESS
CITY   STATE   ZIP

DURING THE TYRANNY OF THE GREEK JUNTA (1968-1974), BRANDING GREECE AS A LAND OF TORTURE, TYRANNY, AND CONCENTRATION CAMPS

During those dark years, few in America would listen to the cries and pain
coming from Greece. The Fascist takeover was condemned by Amnesty International
and a dozen nations in Europe, but not by the United States.
Meanwhile, thousands of heroic Greeks who resisted the junta were being imprisoned.
I ran these ads for the North American Greek Relief Fund to make
Americans understand the tyranny of the junta, and to raise money to help keep
the political prisoners and their families alive. Since 1974,
freedom is back in the birthplace of democracy, and the weeping is over.

THE VIGNELLI CENTER FOR DESIGN PRESENTS

GEORGE
LOIS
(1967)

MASSIMO
VIGNELLI
(1967)

GRECO - ROMAN ADVERTISING & DESIGN WORKSHOP AUGUST 17-19, 2011

**A GREEK AND AN ITALIAN
JOIN FORCES TO TEACH A STUDENT WORKSHOP**

(Massimo and I couldn't resist proving we were studs when we were 36 years-old.)

A LOGO FOR CCNY, WHERE MY ARCHIVES ARE TO BE INSTALLED

For four formative years at the High School of Music & Art in Manhattan
(sadly closed in 1984 due to New York's fiscal emergency),
I would walk past the illustrious campus of CCNY, where I have chosen
to house my archives, and designed this logo in their honor.
It feels like I'm going home.

TRYING TO *UNBRAND* MYSELF AS "THE ORIGINAL MAD MAN"

I resent being called the "Original Mad Man." Here's why:
The 1960s was a heroic age in the history of the art of communication – the audacious
movers and shakers of those times bear no resemblance to the
cast of characters in *Mad Men*. This maddening show is nothing more than a soap opera,
set in a glamorous office where stylish fools hump their appreciative,
coiffured secretaries, suck up martinis, and smoke themselves to death as they produce dumb,
lifeless advertising – oblivious to the inspiring Civil Rights movement,
the burgeoning Women's Lib movement, the evil Vietnam War, and other seismic changes
during the turbulent, roller-coaster 1960s that altered America forever.

**Besides, when I was in my 30s,
I was better looking than Don Draper.**

JON HAMM
AS DON DRAPER

GEORGE LOIS
AS GEORGE LOIS
(1964)

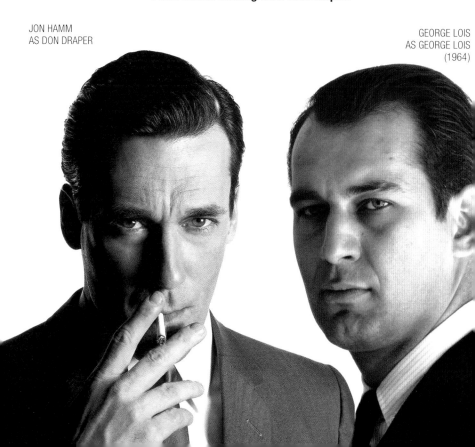

GEORGE LOIS
1960

GEORGE AND LUKE LOIS AT ROCHESTER INSTITUTE OF TECHNOLOGY
WHEN LUKE WAS ATTENDING AS A JUNIOR, 1983

LOIS (ON OTHER) LOGOS
WITH CONCEPTUAL IMAGERY

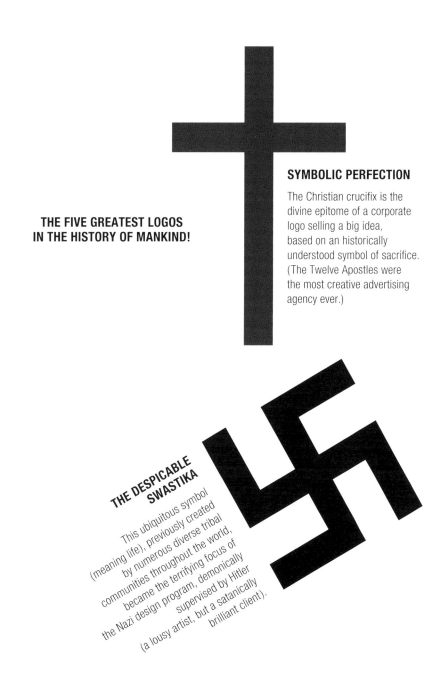

**THE FIVE GREATEST LOGOS
IN THE HISTORY OF MANKIND!**

SYMBOLIC PERFECTION

The Christian crucifix is the
divine epitome of a corporate
logo selling a big idea,
based on an historically
understood symbol of sacrifice.
(The Twelve Apostles were
the most creative advertising
agency ever.)

**THE DESPICABLE
SWASTIKA**

This ubiquitous symbol
(meaning life), previously created
by numerous diverse tribal
communities throughout the world,
became the terrifying focus of
the Nazi design program, demonically
supervised by Hitler
(a lousy artist, but a satanically
brilliant client).

THE STAR OF DAVID

Dating back to antiquity, the Magen David, or "Shield of David," with its two crossed equilateral triangles, is believed to symbolize God, world, man…and creation, revelation, redemption. Classical in form and resonant with historical meaning, its visibility as the logo of modern Israel gives it stirring power and drama, although a hated symbol in much of the Islamic world.

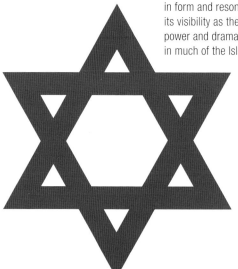

THE ETERNAL EYE

Bill Golden's iconic, all-seeing eye never blinks and certainly never tires. Golden spotted an "Eye of God," somewhat crudely penned on a Shaker birth certificate reproduced in *Antiques* magazine, and Kurt Weihs magnificently designed the pluperfect CBS Television logo.

AND THE MOST MISUNDERSTOOD SYMBOL ON EARTH

The Crescent moon and star symbol, essentially an ancient pagan logo, is the misunderstood symbol of Islam. The symbol became affiliated with the Muslim world when it was adopted by the Ottoman Empire, and subsequently on flag of various Arabic states. But the faith of Islam has historically adopted no symbol, believing that god, and the word of god, cannot be represented by a symbol created by man.

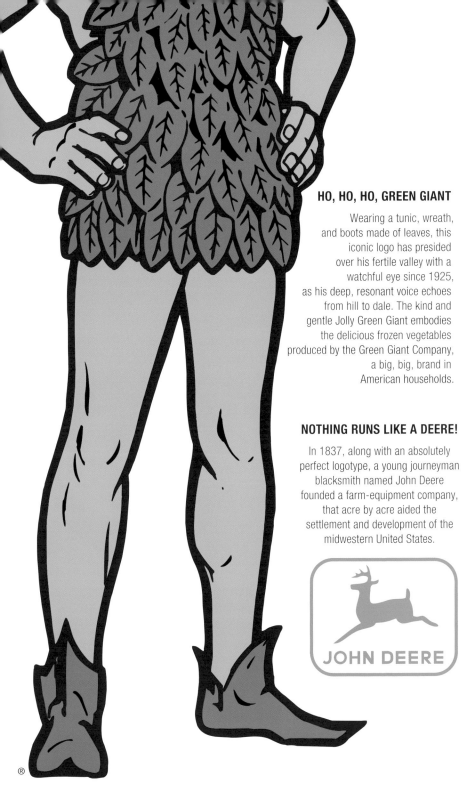

HO, HO, HO, GREEN GIANT

Wearing a tunic, wreath, and boots made of leaves, this iconic logo has presided over his fertile valley with a watchful eye since 1925, as his deep, resonant voice echoes from hill to dale. The kind and gentle Jolly Green Giant embodies the delicious frozen vegetables produced by the Green Giant Company, a big, big, brand in American households.

NOTHING RUNS LIKE A DEERE!

In 1837, along with an absolutely perfect logotype, a young journeyman blacksmith named John Deere founded a farm-equipment company, that acre by acre aided the settlement and development of the midwestern United States.

JOHN DEERE

LOOK FOR THIS LOGO SHINING IN THE NIGHT SKY

Having made his D.C. Comics debut in 1939, Batman survives, more popular than ever, as the star of one of the highest-grossing movie series in history.

ALL OTHER INSURANCE COMPANIES ARE ALL WET

The red Travelers umbrella is one of the great American business icons, a symbol of insurance protection for home, auto, and business.

POKE THIS LOGO IN THE TUMMY AND IT GIGGLES

The Pillsbury Doughboy took his soft-sell approach for ready-to-bake dough to TV in 1965. He walked, talked, and bounced right back when a finger poked his tummy, becoming housewives' favorite in-house chef.

THE RACY LOGO

Since 1926, this streamlined logo depicted the fastest breed of canine used in racing, helping make Greyhound the largest intercity passenger-bus carrier in the world.

GREYHOUND

A FROZEN FOOD LOGO TAKES OFF

When you crave fresh fruits and veggies in the middle of the winter, you can thank Clarence Birdseye for providing the next best thing. In 1922 Clarence invented flash-freezing, so food products could be preserved without altering their taste. Birds Eye – and convenient, delicious frozen food – have been synonymous ever since.

THE FIRST ICONIC FOOD LOGO IN AMERICA

was the instantly recognizable Quaker man, introduced in 1887. The patriarchal Quaker was a homespun image seen as upholding values of honesty and fair trading. On a cold morning, a hot bowl of Quaker Oats still brings a smile to your face.

I'D WALK A MILE FOR A CAMEL

Camel remained one of the top cigarette brands since it was introduced in 1913. R.J. Reynolds named their brand Camel as an illusion to the Turkish tobacco they contained (even though the camel is shown against an Egyptian backdrop). After hundreds of thousands of deaths later, the current design remains basically unchanged.

BULLS-EYE!

The Target logo zeros in on upscale, trend forward merchandise offered at low cost. Using their bulls-eye logo to perfection in advertising and promotion, Target has become the cool, mass-shopping destination for Americans who buy for taste as well as price.

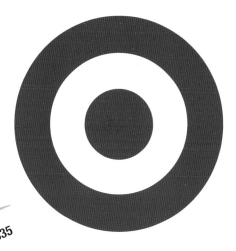

A LEGENDARY LOGO: COST, $35

The legendary Swoosh symbol of Nike (named after the winged Greek goddess of victory – an appropriate name and symbol for athletic shoes) was created in a contest in 1971 by a Portland State University student who was awarded a whopping $35.

THE HORNY PLAYBOY BUNNY

wearing a tuxedo (along with naked women and good writing) have kept *Playboy* magazine a world famous brand name for over a half century.

THE INSTANTLY ICONIC LOGO

In 1984, with an instantly iconic logo, Steve Jobs marketed the Apple Macintosh Home Computer, superb in design and revolutionary in ease-of-use. There's no place like home.

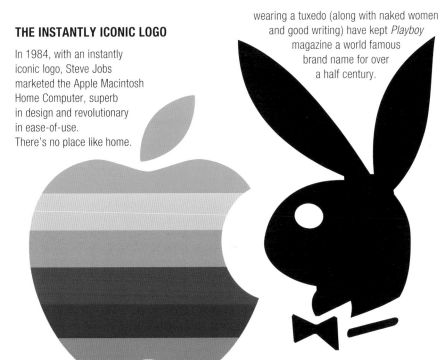

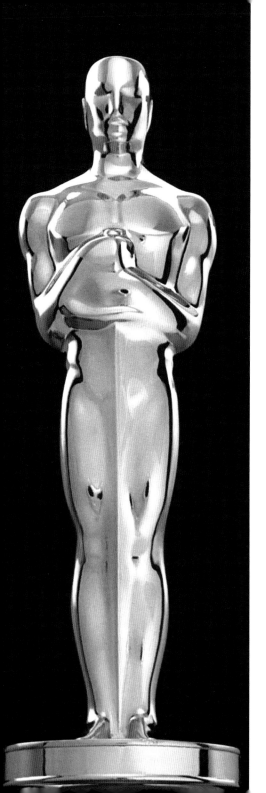

THE WORLD'S MOST COVETED FILM AWARD

The Oscar, the most famous and sought-after award in American popular culture, was designed in 1928 by the modern architect and set designer Cedric Gibbons: a gold-plated robot rising out of a film-reel can, a quintessential American Machine Age design. The statuette got its brand name from a librarian at the Academy of Motion Picture Arts and Sciences, who called it Oscar, because it reminded her of her Uncle Oscar. After a few years of staff members jokingly referring to the award as "Oscar" the name stuck and the golden man was officially branded Oscar by the Academy in 1939.

THE WORLD'S MOST FAMOUS LOGOTYPE

The iconic Coca-Cola logotype and contour bottle was designed in 1915, its shape based on a drawing by an unknown designer of a cocoa bean in an encyclopedia. The memorable bottle shape, the graceful logo, and the pizzazz of sweetness (yuch) and bubbles make Coca-Cola, still, America's favorite soft drink.

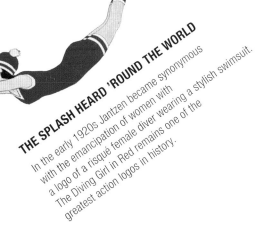

THE SPLASH HEARD 'ROUND THE WORLD

In the early 1920s Jantzen became synonymous with the emancipation of women with a logo of a risqué female diver wearing a stylish swimsuit. The Diving Girl in Red remains one of the greatest action logos in history.

AMERICA'S MAIN SQUEEZE

In 1907, the Sunkist Growers, a marketing cooperative owned by 6,000 citrus growers in California and Arizona, wrapped their oranges in tissue with their Sunkist logo, the first branded fruit in America. In 1926, the Sunkist logo was stamped on every succulent orange, a brilliant and costly idea, a defining moment in American branding history – the first word many children first learned to read while sitting at the breakfast table.

"OUR L'EGGS FIT YOUR LEGS"

In 1970, Herb Lubalin designed the L'eggs logo
that incorporated two egg shaped letters,
boldly positioned on an egg-shaped package containing
a compressed pair of panty hose. L'eggs
revolutionized the industry by being the first hosiery
brand to gain national distribution.

SPOT THE LUCKY ARROW IN THE FED EX LOGO

When I speak of the directional arrow lurking in the Fed Ex logo,
the usual response is, "what arrow?" When Lindon Leader
designed the logo in 1994, he indeed found it to be an incredibly
lucky accident – a gift delivered from the heavens.

GOD CREATES DINOSAURS. GOD DESTROYS DINOSAURS.

From an iconic novel written by Michael Crichton, with an iconic book jacket
designed by Chip Kidd, evolving into a blockbuster
movie directed by Steven Spielberg,
Jurassic Park sparked serious debate on
the plausibility of cloning dinosaurs
(as if the world didn't have
enough problems!).

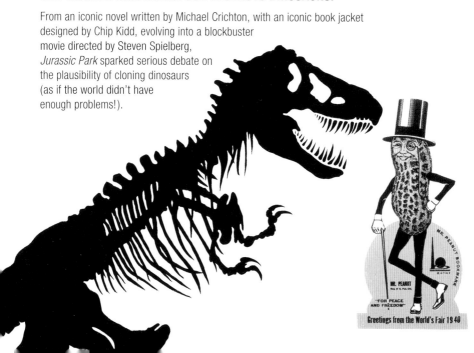

LEVIT & LOIS, IMMORTALIZED BY RAND

In 1993, the legendary Paul Rand designed this dynamic coupling of my name
with that of Herschel Levit, my teacher and mentor at Pratt Institute
(who threw me out of school by getting me a dream job in 1950 designing for
Reba Sochis, yet another beloved mentor). The Paul Rand embossed
design was created for The Herschel Levit Scholarship Dinner that I organized
in Herschel Levit's honor.

THE FIRST NFL HELMET LOGO (FOR THE CLEVELAND RAMS) WAS THE VERY BEST EVER DESIGNED!

In the mid-40's, Rams coach Bob Snyder suggested that running back Fred Gehrke
paint a helmet with Ram horns and show it to owner Dan Reeves – who
then asked Gehrke to paint 75 helmets (for $1 per helmet).
When the helmets debuted during a pre-season game
at the Los Angeles Coliseum, 105,000 people
roared and gave it a standing ovation.

ARE YOU GUYS NUTS?!

Based on a drawing by a Virginia schoolboy
who won a $5 prize in a 1916 contest
for his "little peanut person," Mr. Peanut, sporting
his top hat, spats, cane, white gloves
and monocle, debuted in 1918 in an ad in
The Saturday Evening Post. In 2006,
some execs at Planters conducted an online
poll to determine whether any changes
should be made to Mr. Peanut's stylish dress.
America's answer? "Are you guys nuts?!"

THE PSYCHOTIC LOGO

A classic film logo created in 1960 by the multi-talented designer,
Tony Palladino, one of the stunning young New York
design talents that flowered in the 1960s. His iconic *Psycho* film
logo immediately communicated the psychosis of the
murderous Norman Bates as he acts, talks, and dresses
like his deceased mother, his split personality
dominated by her persona.

THE CANDY AMERICA WENT OVERBOARD FOR
Lifesavers were first created in 1912, but alas,
too late to help rescue the 1,522 doomed passengers
on the ill-fated R.M.S Titanic. The original
five-flavor roll appeared in 1935. The delicious candy
with the hole in the middle came in five flavors,
but America's number one pick was cherry (because
it was the first one on both ends).

OLD ENGLISH GOES MODERN

Derived from the masthead of *The New York Times*, the old English T logo was dramatically transformed by the talented *New York Times Style Magazine* designers into a modern, cutting edge of excellence. Inexplicably, this classic design was replaced in 2014 by a bland, generic, lifeless sans serif T.

THE ICONIC SYMBOL OF MERCY

The logotype for the American Red Cross, established in 1881 by the legendary Clara Barton, is a humanitarian organization that provides emergency assistance, disaster relief, services that help the needy, support for military members and their families, blood collection and distribution, first aid and lifeguard training, and international relief services. The powerful, ubiquitous red cross has become the welcoming symbol of mercy throughout the world.

DUBO, DUBON, DUBONNET

Many of the posters of A.M. Cassandre were so communicative and memorable
that the images he created served as powerful brand logos.
His 1932 Dubonnet man, displayed as a triptych in the streets of Paris,
step by step filling his empty body as he pours and sips aperitif,
has become a popular cultural icon in the modern graphic arts world.

WE ALL ♥ THIS LOGO

The *I love New York* logo, designed in 1977 by
Milton Glaser for the New York State
Department of Economic Development, has
become a part of the American pop
cultural cannon. Any tourist who doesn't take
home a t-shirt with this logo on it,
just doesn't love NY.

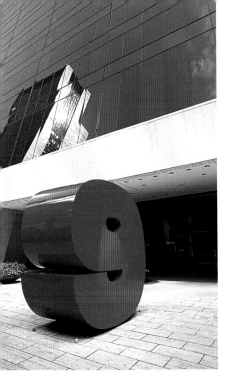

MANHATTAN'S LANDMARK LOGO

The pièce de résistance of the ski-sloped modernist Solow Building at 9 West 57th Street, designed by Gordon Bunshaft of Skidmore, Owings & Merrill, is a monumental ten-foot, 3-dimensional, bright red numeral nine, sitting on a pristine travertine sidewalk, proudly announcing its iconic address. The dramatic concept and design, by the Chermayeff & Geismar design company in 1972, has become a landmark street sculpture, both functional and urban visual entertainment.

THE DISEMBODIED MOVIE SYMBOL

Anatomy of a Murder is one of Saul Bass' most celebrated movie logos and title sequences (also check out The Man with the Golden Arm) for probably the finest courtroom melodrama ever made.

In 1959, for a film with adult subject matter, slicing a male body into seven parts metaphorically introduces subject matter that challenged the arcane censorship guidelines at that time.

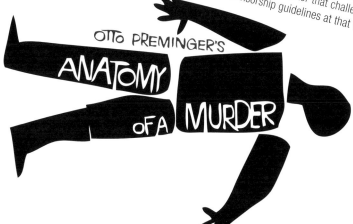

LOOK – AN ICON IN THE SKY!

Since 1925, The Goodyear Blimp, branding and promoting The Goodyear Tire & Rubber Company, has adorned the blue skies of America.

A SHELL OF A LOGO

In 1833, a young man named Marcus Samuel had an import business selling seashells to London collectors. When collecting in the Caspian Sea area in 1892, his son Marcus (Jr.) realized the potential of extracting oil from the region and commissioned the world's first oil tanker – the beginning of the big idea that became The Shell Oil Company. The familiar scallop shell logo was first used in 1904, and the famed industrial designer Raymond Loewy spruced it up in 1971.

"OWN A PIECE OF THE ROCK"

Prudential was founded in 1875 to sell burial insurance. Since then, the company, with its famous logo of the Rock of Gibraltar and its memorable slogan, has become a gigantic financial-services company.

THE LOGO OF CHAMPIONS

The brute appeal of the world-famous Louisville Slugger, from the knob to steady the grip, its tapered handle swelling to display the branded label, growing into the "sweet spot" on the potent barrelhead – one of the most splendidly tailored tools in all of sports. Today there are additional bat brands, but the name Louisville Slugger remains iconic.

M-I-C-K-E-Y-M-O-U-S-E,
MICKEY MOUSE!

Brought to life by Walt Disney, the American entertainment genius,
Mickey Mouse is the most beloved cartoon character of all time.
Mickey Mouse is genuine, cheerful, enthusiastic, humble, confident, versatile,
adventurous, clever, charismatic, and warm – not only the
branding for the Walt Disney Company, but a glowing symbol of America.

THE SPARK OF CREATIVITY

This powerful 1914 poster
by Lucian Bernhard for
the Bosch lighting company
became synonymous
with Bosch, proving once again
that a truly great
poster is a disguised logotype.

A VISUAL SYMBOL MADE IT
THE MOST RECOGNIZABLE PLANE EVER

The Flying Tigers were a heroic volunteer group that flew in Burma and China against the Japanese during the year prior to December 7, 1941. In the first year after the Pearl Harbor attack, they shot down 229 Japanese planes. The shark-faced Curtiss P-40 Warhawk fighter is a true graphic icon in the history of America.

BUSTER BROWN...STILL AROUND!

The branding of the mischievous Buster with his dog Tige, made every kid in America crave Buster Brown shoes. The Buster Brown and Tige logo came to life when The Brown Shoe Company sent Buster Brown and Tige to hundreds of towns across the country from 1904 to 1930. Hundreds of children and grown-ups flocked to see the popular Sunday comic strip character in the flesh. Buster and Tige performed tricks, showed movies, gave away souvenirs, and moms responded when their kids walked home in new pairs of Buster Brown shoes.

HIS MASTER'S VOICE

The RCA Victor logo on this 1917 "Jass" record was the most famous logo in the world before Coca-Cola came along. Nipper doggedly listened to "His Master's Voice" on every RCA Victor product and recording. The original painting was sort of a mourning piece in memory of the brother of the artist, who depicted his brother's dog, Nipper, listening rapturously to the sound of his departed brothers' voice.

THE DUMBEST LOGO "DESIGN" IN AMERICAN HISTORY

The Declaration of Independence, signed in 1776, is a startling document. Of the 56 signatures of our founding fathers, the one of John Hancock was double the size of all the others, and as such, is the most recognized autograph in American history. I assumed that The John Hancock Insurance Company, established in 1862, was denied the usage of the famous signature because of some legal restriction. When I talked to their PR department to verify my assumption, the John Hancock representative said: "Oh no, the company never wanted to seem 'old fashioned,' so we cleaned up his signature so we would have a modern logo." Huh?!

The so-called Liberty Bell was cast in the early 1750s to toll in the Pennsylvania State House. The bell's symbolic meaning is totally misunderstood today. The truth is that the bell only achieved iconic status when, in 1839, Abolitionist's adapted it as a symbol and logotype in its militant literature during their struggle to bring liberty to America's slaves, and gave it the name Liberty Bell. As for the legendary crack, it seems the bell was a lemon – broken on the first stroke of the clapper in 1753!

Looking back, the cracked Liberty Bell was a ringing metaphorical branding of a country breaking apart with a civil war being fought for the freedom of its African-American slaves.

THE ICONIC SYMBOL IN THE STRUGGLE TO BRING LIBERTY TO AMERICA'S SLAVES

"THE MOST FAMOUS POSTER IN THE WORLD" MADE UNCLE SAM SYNONYMOUS WITH THE U.S.

Again, proof that a truly great poster can become an inspiring logotype. James Montgomery Flagg's personification of a stern Uncle Sam (where he based the likeness on himself to "save modeling fees") helped ship American troops into the trenches of WWI, where we had casualties of over 323,000 young Doughboys.

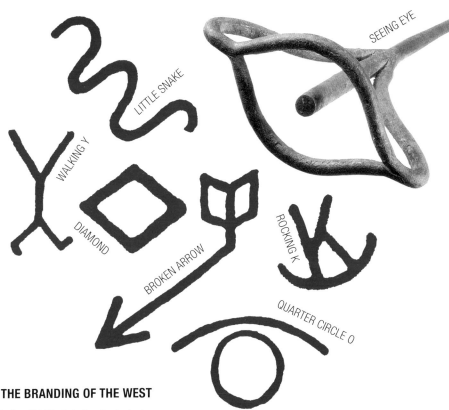

LITTLE SNAKE

SEEING EYE

WALKING Y

DIAMOND

BROKEN ARROW

ROCKING K

QUARTER CIRCLE O

THE BRANDING OF THE WEST

In the Old West, before barbed wire, horses and cows from different ranches grazed together on the open range. To identify its rightful owner, each animal had a mark called a brand burned into its skin with a hot iron. There were countless brands, usually designed by the ranch owner or top hand, made up of symbols, letters, numbers, and geometric shapes. Cattle brands are the precursors of the millions of logotypes that clearly and succinctly identify a company and/or a product.

THERE'S A FORD IN YOUR FUTURE

Ford's first Chief Engineer and Designer, Childe Harold Wills, developed the stylized Ford script, a standard typeface in 1903. An oval was added later, and since 1928 there has been no change in the iconic trademark. It's been a long time since the Model T days (1909-1927) when Henry Ford told us you could chose any color you wanted, "as long as it's black." Today the Ford name lives on in renewed glory for being the only major American automaker to avoid bankruptcy and spurn a government bailout (and lift itself out of fiscal disaster on its own initiative).

THE ICONIC WINGED STEED

The ancient Greeks wrote that the mythological Pegasus sprang from the blood of Medusa when Perseus decapitated her. The winged horse reappeared in the late 19th century when Standard Oil Company of New York (SOCONY) used the inspirational, immortal Pegasus as a logotype to identify gas stations in the U.S. and around the world. SOCONY became Mobil in 1954, and the swift-winged steed still soars above Mobile service stations and on most packaged products.

LIFE GIVES BIRTH
TO THE WORLD OF JOURNALISM

In 1936 Henry Luce, the publisher of *Fortune* and *Time*, created the greatest weekly magazine in history, with a simple, powerful logotype at the top left-hand corner of his revolutionary publication. *Life* spawned many imitations, such as *Look*, but Luce's lineup of legendary photographers dazzled the eye and the mind, week after week, and *Life* dominated the news-magazine category for more than 40 years.

A LOGO HELPED A MIDNIGHT
CULT MOVIE RUN AMOK

The Rocky Horror Picture Show is a science-fiction/horror/comedy/musical film that was released in 1975, had a 30-week first run, and went on to become the cult hit that wouldn't go away, playing weekly midnight shows in theaters all over the country. Any showing is a hallucinatory happening, the cult-film phenomenon of all time, and its lip-biting, type-bleeding logo remains indelibly etched in the annals of American counterculture.

AN ICONIC FIRST COVER BRANDS A MAGAZINE FOREVER

In 1925, the premiere issue of *The New Yorker* magazine sported a cover-illustration drawn
by their art editor, Rea Irvin, of a dandy peering at a butterfly through a monocle,
based on a 1834 caricature of the preening Count D'Orsay. The gent on the original cover is now
referred to as Eustace Tilley, a character created for the magazine as a sort
of roving reporter. Mister Tilley was originally a kind of mascot for *The New Yorker*, and has
become a treasured logotype of the most consistently great
magazines in American history.

WORRYING ABOUT THE BOMB

Designed by Charles Coiner in 1939,
The Civil Defense logo became
ubiquitous in America – a stark, even
forbidding design that symbolized the Cold War,
when school air-raid drills were
conducted in which children were taught to
"duck and cover" under
their desks to avoid atomic fallout.

AN ELECTRIC ICON

Founded in 1886, Westinghouse Electric
helped build America by
pioneering long-distance power and
high-voltage transmissions.
Their logo, designed by Paul Rand in
1960, suggests a printed circuit,
an electrical receptacle, or a face.
Take your pick.

ONE OF THE MOST
VISUAL SYMBOLS IN AMERICAN
POPULAR CULTURE

The Trylon and Perisphere, an enormous,
white futuristic temple, became the
awe-inspiring centerpiece, architectural
symbol, and logotype, designed
by Wallace Harrison and André Fouilhoux
for the 1939-40 New York World's Fair.
It symbolized a beacon of hope
for a nation that endured one storm
of conflict, the Depression,
as we were about to enter yet another,
WWII. The 1939-40 New York
World's Fair, and its inspiring logo,
remains the stuff of memories.
The official fair poster to the right
was designed by Joseph Binder.

TO BOLDLY GO
WHERE NO MAN HAS GONE BEFORE

A logo for the National Aeronautics and
Space Administration with
imagery of their tremendous technical
and scientific accomplishments –
demonstrating vividly that humans can achieve
previously inconceivable feats.

"HELLO? MA BELL? ARE YOU THERE?"

The Bell name and logo were conceived
in 1889, named after Alexander Graham Bell,
the inventor of the telephone.
In 1984, the "Bell System," along with
its redesigned logo by
Saul Bass, disappeared from the
American landscape.
But the company's old nickname,
"Ma Bell," still rings true.

THE LOGO THAT NEVER WEARS OUT

The Michelin Man (aka Monsieur Bibendum), designed
by the poster artist O'Galop in 1898, based
on tires stacked up in assorted sizes, provides instant
identity and a fun-loving graphic tool that drives
their advertising and
promotion.

WHEN IT RAINS IT POURS

Since 1914 the Morton Salt
Umbrella Girl has been walking
in the rain, accidentally
pouring salt, charmingly driving
home the point that Morton
salt flowed freely in damp weather.
She remains an enduring
logotype on Morton packaging.

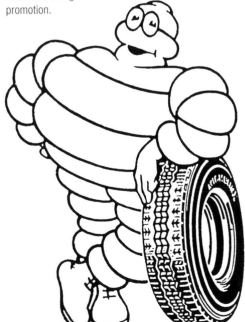

BRANDING THE UPCOMING AMERICAN REVOLUTION

In 1754, twenty years before the outbreak of the American Revolution, Benjamin Franklin urged the American colony to prepare for its own defense against both French and Indian forces on the frontier, who continually attacked the American subjects of Great Britain. The mother country appeared incapable or unwilling to protect them. Franklin's brilliant design, *Join, or Die*, appeared in his *Pennsylvania Gazette*, and called for the delegates to the Albany convention of 1754 to organize an inter-colonial council for defense, with taxing powers, an American army, fortifications, an expansion plan, and a Crown-appointed presiding officer. Every colony rejected his plan. Franklin believed until his death that if it had been adopted, it would have prevented the need for the American Revolution. Blimey!

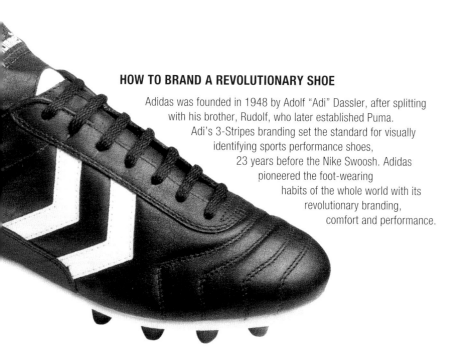

HOW TO BRAND A REVOLUTIONARY SHOE

Adidas was founded in 1948 by Adolf "Adi" Dassler, after splitting with his brother, Rudolf, who later established Puma. Adi's 3-Stripes branding set the standard for visually identifying sports performance shoes, 23 years before the Nike Swoosh. Adidas pioneered the foot-wearing habits of the whole world with its revolutionary branding, comfort and performance.

Soaring to Success !

Daily Herald

— the Early Bird.

AN HAUTE LOGO

The mere use of initials by
a logo designer,
when not based on an idea,
no matter how well
designed, never gives me
a thrill. But this 1963
logotype by A. M. Cassandre
of the initials of
Yves Saint Laurent's luxury
fashion house, seems
to be the epitome of elegance,
instantly triggering
recognition and a haute-couture ethos.

A MODERN NEW LOOK IN BRANDING

This 1916 imagery of the movement of a bird formation
in flight was originally designed by the American-born
Brit, E. McKnight Kauffer, as a modernist graphic design.
In 1919, the editor of the *Daily Herald*, a Labour
newspaper, adapted Kauffer's image and was captioned
"Soaring to Success! – the Early Bird," a metaphor
for the recent invention of "aeroplanes," a symbol of hope
in those desperate days of WWI. The poster became
a revolutionary branding symbol for the newspaper (as well
as the Labour Party) inspiring Kauffer to go on to
become an internationally acclaimed and influential
poster designer. In 1954, his friend Sabro Hasigawa laid an
origami paper bird on his gravestone.

THE LOGOTYPE THAT BECAME AN INSTANT ICON

In 2003 the Google search engine became a cultural phenomenon and a verb.
To research specific information these days you "google it."
Google has sped up information gathering a thousandfold, achieving preeminent
status as an augmenter of the human brain, able to direct you
to anything you don't know, or have forgotten. (For more info, google Google.)

THE KODAK MOMENT (HAS PASSED)

George Eastman put the first simple camera into the
hands of a new world of image makers in 1888,
making a complicated process simple. For over a century,
amateurs and professional photographers have
relied on Kodak to capture the decisive moment
(until the advent of digital photography).

IT'S AN "I" AND A "P," IT'S AN UPWARD ARROW, IT'S A TREE, IT'S ALL THREE!

In 1960, Lester Beall designed the
International Paper Company trademark,
an I and a P, an uplifting arrow,
that form a tree – an isometric triangle in
a circle, in conceptual harmony.

TAKING A BIG BITE OF THE SPORTSWEAR MARKET

In the late 1920s, tennis pro Jean René Lacoste, a feared
competitor on the courts, was given the nickname
The Crocodile. In 1933, he capitalized on
his fame when he co-founded a sportswear
company and branded it Lacoste, and
Robert George designed one of the most
recognized logos in the world.

In 1963, Seymour Chwast's branding of an "A" for Artone, in a fluid Art Nouveau lettering form, has always felt viscerally perfect for the supplier of an India Ink product, a widely used form of ink used by graphic artists, including Seymour and his fellow Push Pin Studios' designers.

A FREE FLOWING LOGOTYPE FOR AN INDIA INK SUPPLIER

A LOGO FOR A COMPANY THAT HAS EARNED FIVE NOBEL PRIZES

IBM is a worldwide information-technology leader, and the only one with a continuous history dating back to the 19th century. This simple, bold, fresh logo for Big Blue was designed by Paul Rand in 1972, after a redesign of a simpler version he created in 1956. Eight stripes radiate throughout the logo to offer a dazzling visual effect suggesting speed and dynamism, making it one of the most recognized logotypes in the world (and a design that has been imitated ad nauseam by hack designers since).

MAKE LOVE NOT WAR

was the rallying cry for youthful antiwar activists
during the Vietnam War, used on
protest signs, posters, and buttons in the U.S.
Along with the worldwide Peace symbol,
which was originally designed as a logo for the
Campaign for Nuclear Disarmament,
it became the slogan for American counterculture
during the Age of Aquarius.

THE ANIMATED BRANDING
OF A LIFELESS CIGAR

In 1952, Paul Rand took an El Producto cigar,
gave it a hat and hands, and by using an
animated cigar in dozens of ads, visual branding
was born. Rand, the first great modernist
designer, wrote: "A trademark is not merely a
device to adorn a letterhead, to stamp a
product, or to insert at the base of an ad…when
fully exploited the trademark can
actively stimulate interest in the product or brand."

ALL ABOARD THE NEW HAVEN RAILROAD

In 1955 the Swiss-born designer
Herbert Matter created an energetic logo for
The New Haven Railroad, inspired by
the crossing of a maze of tracks intersecting
each other in a railway yard.

THE TOP BANANA OF FRUIT LOGOS

The Golden Age of Advertising Jingles is long gone,
but some keep coming back like a song.
One of the most memorable of the golden oldies
is the 1944 jingle sung by an animated
Miss Chiquita logotype, a Carmen Miranda look-alike banana,
who taught Americans how to ripen and
use bananas (preferably the Chiquita brand).

I'm Chiquita Banana and I've come to say
Bananas have to ripen in a certain way
When they are fleck'd with brown and have a golden hue
Bananas taste the best and are best for you
You can put them in a salad
You can put them in a pie-aye
Any way you want to eat them
It's impossible to beat them
But, bananas like the climate of the very, very tropical equator
So you should never put bananas in the refrigerator.

OKAY, BETTER, EVEN BETTER, BEST!

A powerful, ultra-simple logotype designed by Chermayeff & Geismar
for Best Products, a catalog showroom retail chain,
that visually reinforces the meaning
of the word, "Best."

BEST

A WARM AND FUZZY WOOLMARK LOGO

Designed by Francesco Saroglio in 1964 for the
International Wool Secretariat,
a stylistic, 3-dimensional ball of wool that
has served as the Woolmark
symbol for over half a century, elegantly signifying
that a retail product contains pure,
new wool.

THEY JUST CAN'T KEEP THEIR HANDS
OFF THIS MERMAID

The original logo for Starbucks, named after
Starbuck, the coffee-loving first mate
in the classic American novel, Moby Dick,
depicted a crowned, bare-breasted
siren, holding her double fishtails, surrounded
by the words Starbucks, Coffee, Tea, Spices.
Then a version where her long locks covered her
once visible nipples, with the words
Starbucks Coffee. Then a close-up of her
(with a missing belly button).
The last version, we hope, is the one above,
sans the brand name all together.
Enough already.

THE OLDEST
(AND ONE OF THE MOST FAMOUS)
AMERICAN BRANDS STILL
IN EXISTENCE

The arm and hammer was originally a
stylized representation of Vulcan, the Roman
God of Fire and metal working, adapted
prior to the American Civil War as a symbol
of the labor movement, and also
used by the Socialist Labor Party of America.
But it also dates back to the 1860s as
a brand name and logo for the Vulcan Spice
Mills, who designed the symbol and
named their baking soda Arm & Hammer.

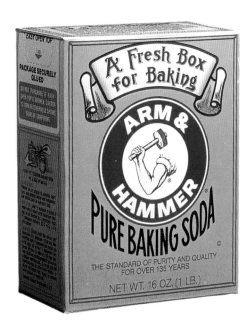

THE MOST FAMOUS SUPERHERO OF ALL TIME

Born on the planet Krypton, Clark Kent, in a claustrophobic phone booth, strips off his white shirt and tie. The world gasps at the sight of the identifying Superman logo on his chest, about to use his superhuman abilities for the benefit of the helpless and the oppressed and defender of the American way of life.

THE BRANDING OF THE BIRTHPLACE OF MODERNISM

The Weiner Werkstätte (the Vienna Workshop) was founded in 1903 by Josef Hoffmann and Koloman Moser, making Vienna the hub of modernist innovation in art, architecture, graphic art and design (including book bindings, furnishings, tableware, jewelry, wallpapers, textiles, and haute couture fashion), that left their mark (and trademark) on the entire 20th century. The Weiner Werkstätte was launched as a dynamic, meticulously proportioned and detailed antidote to over-ornate traditional forms, all under the banner of the no-nonsense, in-your-face WW logo.